ANTISEMITISM

WHAT IT IS. WHAT IT ISN'T.
WHY IT MATTERS.

Julia Neuberger

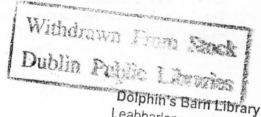

WEIDENFELD & NICOLSON

First published in Great Britain in 2019 by Weidenfeld & Nicolson
an imprint of The Orion Publishing Group Ltd
Carmelite House, 50 Victoria Embankment
London EC4Y 0DZ

An Hachette UK Company

1 3 5 7 9 10 8 6 4 2

A CIP catalogue record for this book
is available from the British Library.

ISBN (paperback) 978 1 4746 1240 1
ISBN (ebook) 978 1 4746 1241 8

Typeset by Input Data Services Ltd, Somerset

Printed and bound in Great Britain by Clays Ltd, Elcograf S.p.A.

www.orionbooks.co.uk

Dedicated to the memory of
George Weidenfeld
(1919–2016)
and
Anna Schwab
(1887–1963)

CONTENTS

INTRODUCTION

When I was a child, growing up in north London, we did not talk about antisemitism. If it came up in conversation, it would likely have been in jest – driving us around in our shabby Ford Popular, my father enjoyed declaring that the traffic lights, when they were red one after the other, were antisemitic. But that was it.

My father's grandmother, Caroline Ellern, had been deported from where she had sought refuge from Nazi Germany, in Amsterdam, to Westerbork and on to Sobibor where she was murdered in 1943. Most of my mother's family had been murdered. And yet ten or fifteen years later, antisemitism was about traffic lights; it was almost a joke. If Jews felt threatened by antisemitism in 1950s or 1960s Britain, we certainly were not aware of it. The horror of the concentration and extermination camps, shown widely on newsreel footage in cinemas immediately after the war, had forced those with antisemitic views to think again, or at least hold their peace.

The Holocaust was discussed very little when I was a child. I grew up surrounded by people with German accents, my mother included (though I could not hear it unless listening to her, in later years, on her voicemail message). Like my mother, I had many cousins, uncles, aunts and friends who fled Nazi Germany. But England, Britain, felt safe. We were proud to be British, proud to be Jewish and we felt unthreatened.

At school, where about a third of the class was Jewish, no fresh subject matter we had not looked at before was covered in lessons held on Jewish High Holy Days. There was no point; too many of us were absent. In what was known as 'united' prayers, the once a week session where we all sang English hymns together – and I still adore them – we were careful to choose those that were suitable for all. Where there was uncertainty, the senior teachers would consult parents, or Jewish staff members. People were sensitive, accepting, tolerant – we never thought it a problem.

I will never know how much my sense of security was down to a deliberate ploy on the part of my parents, to shield me and my cousins from what had happened. After all, my mother had lost out on her education. Though reparation negotiations with the German government were going on in the late 1950s and '60s, I heard little about it. My grandparents had left with virtually nothing, and seeking compensation for their house became an almost full time obsession in the early 1960s. But as children, my cousins and I were 'innocents'; we were safe. We were free to practise Judaism, free to walk round the streets in fancy dress at Purim, free to wear sparkly shoes at Chanukkah. We lit our Chanukkah candles and put them in the window. And nobody turned a hair.

Much later on, when I experienced minute amounts of antisemitism – mostly borne of ignorance – in my student years and beyond, when a few far-right activists were sending offensive cards to prominent Jews, it still felt less than serious. When the Runnymede Trust, a race relations equality organisation, decided to conduct an enquiry into the prevalence of antisemitism as a dry run for an enquiry into what then seemed much more serious, Islamophobia, we did not think we would find much, or that it would be especially disturbing. Our 1994 report, entitled – presciently, as it turned out – 'A Very Light Sleeper', covered early Holocaust denial and offensive letters and cards. It raised some pretty unpleasant examples and caused some alarm, but it did not appear then as serious as the growing phenomenon of Islamophobia.

So why is this worth addressing now? The simple answer is because the music has changed.

I have been deeply disturbed by the rise of antisemitism in Europe over the last fifteen years or so, with its attendant violent attacks on Jewish targets in some places. Verbal antisemitism is also on the rise, with an acceptability in many circles of what would hitherto have been condemned as outrageous antisemitic discourse.

In 2017, the Community Security Trust and the Institute for Jewish Policy Research came together to conduct a major study of antisemitism in the UK. The report found that what it called a 'hard-core' antisemite population was capped at 5 per cent, while it detected 'a further 25 per cent who feel negatively about Jews and hold one or two viewpoints that most Jews would consider antisemitic. These include traditional Judeophobic tropes of undue influence, divided loyalty, and ill-gotten wealth.'[1] The far-right remains the most antisemitic demographic, but the far-left, by the force of numbers and its new-found influence over British politics, was found to be roughly on an even keel with reactionaries when it comes to harbouring anti-Jewish feelings. These figures are alarming. But, though these are important groupings, the most worrying evidence is that antisemitism – or signs of its influence in populations where it never existed – has become quite widespread in British society.

Like the canary singing in the mine, I want to call out the antisemitism that exists now, not because, as yet, it encompasses violent incidents – here in the UK it largely does not – but because violent name-calling has a habit of morphing into violence perpetrated against people or buildings, with desecration of what is regarded as holy or sacrosanct, and the engendering of fear. The appalling shooting, as I was writing this book, at the Etz Chayyim synagogue in Pittsburgh, in the middle of Sabbath services, by a man who believed Jews were responsible for bringing Muslims to America, shouting out 'All Jews must die', is a case in point.

The other reason I feel this book needs to be written is that there is genuine bewilderment among many people as to what antisemitism really is, and particular confusion over whether criticism of the State of Israel is in itself antisemitic. Yet we do now have a generally agreed international definition, even if an imperfect one, one as yet not widely known among the general public. So it is worth setting out what antisemitism is and equally what it is not – not least because there is considerable pain felt by much of the UK Jewish community caused by what they perceive as rising antisemitism, an atmosphere of disquiet, and furthermore a real concern over what is in their view a breach of trust between the nation and its Jewish population, a Jewish community that has felt blessed by its long welcome here, and which, unlike those

4

in much of continental Europe, can boast 350 years and more of proud uninterrupted history in this country.

I want to look at what's been happening to attitudes to Jews. I want to do that because I want to understand it. And I want to understand it because I want to think about the implications not only for my generation of Jews, but also, far more importantly, for the next generation and the one after that. What future do Jews have in Britain, and indeed in Europe, when violence against Jews – both verbal and physical – is on the rise, while all over Europe right-wing nationalists are becoming more and more intolerant, more and more antisemitic and Islamophobic? And what does that mean, not just for Jews, but for society as a whole?

CHAPTER 1

Where did antisemitism come from?

In order to understand the nuances involved in calling out what is – and, crucially, what isn't – antisemitism, it is important to explore where it comes from. To do that we need to go back in history. Not for nothing is antisemitism called 'the longest hatred'. It has its roots in religious anti-Judaism, in tribal wars, in resentment of the very fact of Jews' stubborn survival against the odds, and in a whole variety of other factors. It has combined religious hatred with viewing Jews as less than human, and envy with a view that says Jews cannot have come by whatever success they have had fairly – they are dishonest, usurers, cheats and malevolent. History tells us some of the roots of all this.

The Ancient World

Alexandria, Egypt, in the third century BCE, was home to the largest Jewish diaspora in the world. The Septuagint, a Greek translation of the Hebrew Bible, was produced there. We know that Manetho, an Egyptian priest and historian of that era, wrote scathingly of the Jews. His themes are repeated endlessly, including in the Roman period. In the Seleucid Empire, which stretched from

Anatolia to the Levant, Mesopotamia, and parts of modern Pakistan, one of the earliest anti-Jewish edicts was promulgated by Antiochus IV Epiphanes in about 170–167 BCE, sparking a revolt of the Maccabees in Judea, which is recorded in the Books of Maccabees in the Apocrypha. This is the subject of operas and oratorios, and is of course the origin of the Jewish winter festival of light, Chanukkah.

Antiochus IV reversed the old custom of leaving the Jews of Judea to carry on their religious traditions; provided they paid their taxes, their foreign rulers did not interfere. Instead he persecuted the people for their religious practice, leading to the Maccabean Revolt in 167 BCE. The city of Jerusalem was destroyed, many Jews were slaughtered, and Antiochus established a new military Greek citadel.

Antiochus is the major villain and persecutor in the Jewish traditions associated with Chanukkah, including the Books of Maccabees and the 'Scroll of Antiochus', where the Maccabean Revolt was painted as a national resistance to a foreign political and cultural oppression. The rabbis referred to him as 'the wicked one'. Whether Antiochus's policy was directed at extermination of Judaism as a culture and a religion is unclear, but he was certainly an ancient Judeophobe or antisemite.

Christian Antisemitism: The Early Church

Much later, by the second century CE, early Christians seem to have felt compelled to discredit the status of Jews by emphasising their lack of faith, and their fall from grace, plus their general pig-headedness in refusing either to accept that Jesus was the Messiah or to accept his teachings. Although Jesus' teachings were strongly influenced by Jewish thought, the early church did not accept that he was teaching Judaism. Theirs was the new faith, being taken out beyond Jews to the nations of the known world; the Jews were seen as failures, people who could not see reason.

The major assumption of the new religion, unlike Judaism, was that the Messiah had come in the person of Jesus (Christ) and that the New Age was imminent. The only people allowed to teach the truths of the new religion were students of the apostles. Each apostle specified a student to succeed him. And the Apostolic Line challenged the legitimacy of any group other than itself being the New Israel.

In order to justify their early church doctrine, the Apologists (the new thinkers) vilified the Jews. If Christianity was to be the New Israel, they had to explain the sins of the Old Israel, the fallen Israel, and the false, treacherous Israel.

In 145 CE, Justin Martyr wrote an apology in which he was having a dialogue with a Jew named Trypho. Using Bible proof texts – the traditional way to argue a point in Judaism – Justin Martyr claimed that the Jews were originally selected by God because they were such an unspiritual group, and he then attacked them for rejecting Jesus, for killing Jesus and for leading people away from salvation. He described the destruction of the Temple as being just punishment for Jewish perfidy. His writings had great influence on early Christian thought, and many scholars think that they may have been the origins of Christian antisemitism.

But Justin Martyr was not alone. The Church Fathers identified Jews and Judaism with heresy and declared the people of Israel to be *extra Deum* 'outside of God'. St Peter of Antioch referred to Christians who refused to worship religious images as having 'Jewish minds'. In the early second century CE, the heretic Marcion of Sinope, hugely influential in the early church, declared that the Jewish God was a different God, inferior to the Christian one, and rejected the Jewish scriptures as the product of a lesser deity. Marcion's teachings rejected Judaism not only as an incomplete revelation, but as a false one as well.

Most Christian orthodox authorities argued that Judaism was an incomplete and inferior religion to Christianity, but defended the Jewish scriptures, the Hebrew Bible, as canonical. Origen of Alexandria (c. 184–c. 253) was more knowledgeable about Judaism than any of the other Church Fathers, having studied Hebrew, met Rabbi Hillel the Younger, consulted and debated with Jewish scholars, and been influenced by the allegorical interpretations of Philo of Alexandria. He defended Jews of the past as having been chosen by God for their merits. But he condemned contemporary Jews for not understanding their own Law, insisted that Christians were the 'true Israel', and blamed the Jews for the death of Christ. John Chrysostom (344–407 CE), one of the most important of the Church Fathers, declared that 'The synagogue is worse than a brothel . . . it is the den of scoundrels and the repair of wild beasts.'

Then there is the most famous of them all, St Augustine (c. 354–430 CE), who wrote in his Confessions (12.14):

How hateful to me are the enemies of your Scripture! How I wish that you would slay them [the Jews] with your two-edged sword, so that there should be none to oppose your word! Gladly would I have them die to themselves and live to you![1]

We can find a few – a very few – positive remarks from the Church Fathers about the Jews, but by the tenth and eleventh centuries, vile doctrines about Jews, well known around the Christian world, became hardened and unified. Add to that mix the successive waves of Muslim conquest, leading to the military and spiritual zeal of the Christian Crusades against the Muslims, in which the Jews of Europe became caught up, along with the growth of Christianity in northern Europe, and you have a perfect situation for Jews to be persecuted almost everywhere they lived in Europe, as of course they were.

In the medieval period, Judaism became the only persistent minority religion within the by then wholly Christian continent of Europe, once both Jews and Muslims had been expelled from Spain, and paganism had been wiped out. While Jews could be and were welcomed from time to time in one city state or another, at a time when one's faith was perceived as the principal form of self-identity, Jews found themselves increasingly isolated as outsiders.

Christian Antisemitism: The High Middle Ages

In the Gospel of Matthew, when Pilate declared himself innocent of Jesus' death, it is said, 'And all the people answered, "His blood be on us and on our children!"'[2]

11

Over the course of time, and certainly by the Middle Ages, Christians began to accept this interpretation of the crucifixion – that the Jewish people as a whole were responsible for killing Jesus, that both the Jews present at Jesus' death and the Jewish people collectively and for all time, have committed the sin of *deicide*, or God-killing.

In medieval Europe, Easter week in particular was a time of great danger for Jews, and they were frequently attacked. They were also forced by church decree to wear a special hat or badge so they were instantly recognisable. The Nazis invented nothing new with the yellow star.

For 1,900 years of Christian-Jewish history, the charge of *deicide* has led to hatred, violence against and murder of Jews in Europe and worldwide.[3] The accusation was finally repudiated in 1964, when the Catholic Church under Pope Paul VI issued the document *Nostra aetate* as a part of the Second Vatican Council. Despite that, there is still widespread belief among some groups that Jews are Christ killers.

Christian Antisemitism: The Blood Libel

In England in 1144, the Jews of Norwich were accused of ritual murder after a boy, William of Norwich, was found dead with stab wounds in the woods. It was claimed around this time that every year an international council of Jews would choose a country where a child would be killed during Easter week, in order to make unleavened bread for Passover (which usually coincides with Easter), because – so the antisemites claimed – of what is in fact a non-existent Jewish prophecy that states that the killing of a Christian child each year will ensure that the Jews will be restored to the Holy Land. According to this outlandish story, in 1144 England was chosen, and the leaders of the Jewish community delegated the Jews of Norwich to perform the abduction and killing of William.

It may have been arrant nonsense, but it did not stop similar accusations in other towns and cities. In 1189, the Jewish deputation attending the coronation of Richard the Lionheart was attacked, and massacres of Jews in London and York soon followed.

After the death of another child, Hugh of Lincoln, there were trials and executions of Jews. It was not long afterwards, in 1290, that the Jews were expelled from England, not to be readmitted until 1656.

From around the twelfth century until the mid-nineteenth century, there were Christians throughout Europe who claimed that some (or all) Jews possessed magical powers, which, some believed, were gained from making a deal with the devil; ideas of Jews having horns or tails were commonplace. On the bridge by the gates to the Frankfurt ghetto, where my paternal ancestors would have lived, there was a large depiction of the so-called *Judensau*, Jewish pig – an image that began to appear in the medieval period, and was often accompanied by antisemitic commentary.

The city of Wittenberg in Germany still has a *Judensau*, dating from 1305, on the facade of the Stadtkirche where Martin Luther, the founder of the Protestant Church, preached. It portrays a rabbi who looks under the sow's tail, with other Jews drinking from its teats. It is one of the last remaining examples in Germany depicting medieval 'Jew baiting'. Luther described the *Judensau* sculpture at Wittenberg – the Rabbi bent over the sow 'lifting up her right leg, holding her tail high and looking intensely under her tail and into her Talmud, as though he were reading something acute or extraordinary'.[4]

Luther was known to be a ferocious antisemite who ranted about what Christians ought to do with 'this damned, rejected race of Jews', declaring that 'we cannot tolerate them if we do not wish to share in their lies, curses, and blasphemy.' He was quite clear in setting out what he really thought should happen to the Jews in a pamphlet in which he suggested setting synagogues on fire, breaking down and destroying Jewish homes and putting Jews 'under one roof or in a stable, like gypsies', depriving them of their prayer-books and Talmuds, forbidding rabbis to teach under threat of death, forbidding travelling privileges – all in the interests of being free of 'this insufferable devilish burden – the Jews'.[5]

And the objections to the Jews continued. In 1819, just as the emancipation of the Jews was beginning in parts of Europe, including parts of Germany, the so-called 'Hep hep riots' took place. (Hep hep is probably a shepherd's call to his flock, but some have argued that it stands for *Hierosolyma est Perdita*, Jerusalem is lost.) The Jews were portrayed as 'upstarts' attempting to take control of the economy, particularly the financial sector, and antisemitic publications became common in the German press. Amos Elon writes of this period:

In some places, attempts were made to return Jews to their old medieval status. The free city of Frankfurt re-instated parts of the medieval statute that restricted the rights of Jews. As of 1816 only twelve Jewish couples were allowed to marry each year . . . In the Rhineland, which had reverted to Prussian control, Jews lost the citizenship rights they had been granted under the French and were no longer allowed to practice certain professions. The few who had been appointed to public office before the war were summarily dismissed.[6]

And alongside all this, there were physical attacks, looting, and much destruction of property belonging to Jews. The Nazi creation of Kristallnacht had an ancestor of sorts.

In Germany and elsewhere, the blood libel has occasionally been repeated in modern times – since the Second World War – by extreme antisemites, and it can be found remarkably frequently on social media these days. Accusations of the Jews' responsibility for the death of Christ were also reasonably commonplace until the 1960s.

Some myths are hard to dispel, and no doubt they have their spill-over now, even though most churches would be horrified to be accused of fomenting or indeed even tolerating antisemitism. Many are doing what they can to stamp it out – and have shown great kindness and generosity towards Jews, even altering the liturgy for particular services in order that Jews feel comfortable taking part – but they do not always succeed.

For there is still the vestige of 'religious' antisemitism in some churches, with some still praying for the conversion of the Jews, or believing Judaism to be incomplete without Christianity. For many Christians, Judaism is the religion of the Old Testament (Hebrew Bible) because they know nothing of the development of rabbinic Judaism in parallel with the beginnings of the Christian church and beyond. Organisations such as the Council of Christians and Jews or the Woolf Institute have been set up to promote Jewish-Christian understanding, but they have a difficult row to hoe due to the ignorance around what Judaism is and how it has both considerable similarities with and major differences from Christianity. And ignorance can and does breed prejudice, and even contempt.

Islamic Antisemitism Until the Late Nineteenth Century

There are differing opinions among scholars, but most agree that the majority of discrimination against non-Muslims was not specifically targeted at Jews, but at all non-believers. Bernard Lewis, a great scholar of medieval and modern Islam, even argues that while Muslims may have held negative stereotypes regarding Jews throughout most of Islamic history, these stereotypes were different from European antisemitism because Muslims viewed Jews as objects of ridicule, not fear. Lewis argues that Muslims did not attribute 'cosmic evil' to Jews, and that it was not until the late nineteenth century that antisemitic movements first appeared among Muslims that can compare with what occurred in Europe.[7]

There is also considerable disagreement among Jews who were born in Muslim countries as to the historic prevalence of antisemitism, with Edwin Shuker, a vice-president of the Board of Deputies, coming under attack in early November 2018 for arguing, at an event for local councillors, that historically, Arab Jews and Muslims had lived in harmony and the 'first time that harmony was disturbed was in the 1940s'.[8] Others disagreed fundamentally, and pointed to antisemitic occurrences taking place far earlier.[9]

Many scholars argue that modern Islamic antisemitism has been 'caught' from European Christian modes of expression, and that that, combined with rage in the Arab world about the existence of the State of Israel, is now a potent force. But it was not always like this. Historically speaking, the relationship between Jews and Muslims did not start badly. According to Bernard Lewis, the earliest verses of the Quran were largely sympathetic to Jews. Muhammad admired them as monotheists and saw them as natural adherents to the new faith, while Jewish practices helped model early Islamic behaviour, such as midday prayer, prayers on Friday, Ramadan fasting (modelled after the Jewish Yom Kippur fast on the tenth of the month of Tishri), and particularly the fact that until 623 CE Muslims prayed towards Jerusalem, not Mecca.[10]

The 'Constitution of Medina' was drawn up on behalf of the prophet Muhammad shortly after his arrival at Medina (then known as Yathrib) in 622 to establish the collective responsibility of nine constituent tribes for their members' actions. Eight Jewish groups were recognised as part of the Yathrib community, and their religious separation from Muslims was established. The constitution also established Muhammad as the mediating authority between groups and forbade the waging of war without his authorisation. It therefore formed the basis of a multi-religious Islamic state in Medina. The document ensured freedom of religious beliefs and practices for all citizens who 'follow the believers.'

Muhammad upheld the peaceful coexistence of Muslims, Jews and Christians, defining them all, under given conditions, as constituting the *umma*, or community of that city: 'Those Jews who follow us are entitled to our aid and support so long as they shall not have wronged us or lent assistance [to any enemies] against us.'[11]

The Quran also clears Jews from the Christian accusation of *deicide*,[12] though there is a standard negative view of the Jews to be found there too:

And abasement and poverty were pitched upon them, and they were laden with the burden of God's anger; that, because they had disbelieved the signs of God and slain the Prophets unrightfully; that, because they disobeyed, and were transgressors.[13]

However, the Quran as a whole clearly gives some legitimacy to Judaism: 'Those who believe, and the Jews, and the Sabi'un [Sabaeans], and the Christians, who believe in God and the Last Day and do good, there is no fear for them, nor shall they grieve.'[14]

But views expressed about Jews and Judaism did change over the years. There are various versions of a hadith (a later record of the words or actions of the prophet Muhammad) which has been quoted many times, and has become part of the charter of Hamas – the Sunni Muslim fundamentalist organisation that governs Gaza:

The Day of Judgement will not come about until Muslims fight the Jews, when the Jew will hide behind stones and trees. The stones and trees will say O Muslims, O Abdullah, there is a Jew behind me, come and kill him. Only the Gharqad tree [the Boxthorn tree] would not do that because it is one of the trees of the Jews.[15]

There are many different interpretations of what the

Gharqad tree is or was. One is that it is a genuine tree, and that Israelis are alleged to plant that tree around various locations, such as their settlements in West Bank and Gaza. Another interpretation is that the tree is symbolic, rather than real and to be found in nature, and that any reference to it is about all the forces of the world believed to conspire with the Jews against Muslims.[16]

Modern Muslim Antisemitism

In recent decades, broad tolerance within mainstream Islam has begun to change as Islamist thinking gained influence. As early as 1950, the seminal Islamist thinker and Muslim Brotherhood leader Sayyid Qutb was writing about 'Our Struggle With the Jews', claiming: 'World Jewry's purpose is to eliminate all limitations, especially the limitations posed by faith and religion, so that the Jews may penetrate into [the] body politic of the whole world and then may be free to perpetuate their evil designs.' Which could easily have been taken from the Protocols of the Elders of Zion.

The Protocols of the Elders of Zion Reborn

It is certainly true that a quick glance through social media on some Muslim sites, and those of the far-left and far-right brings one to despair about what is being circulated. The plethora of references to the Protocols of the Elders of Zion is deeply depressing, and IsraHell for Israel is common parlance.

The Protocols of the Elders of Zion is an antisemitic text purporting to describe a Jewish plan for global domination and was first published in Russia in 1903. It was then translated into multiple languages and disseminated internationally throughout the early twentieth century, becoming a bestseller. The renowned right-wing antisemite Henry Ford funded the printing of 500,000 copies that were distributed throughout the United States in the 1920s. Some German teachers assigned it as a text to be read by German schoolchildren after the Nazis came to power in 1933. Once described by leading historian Norman Cohn as a 'warrant for genocide',[17] the Protocols were used by the Nazis as propaganda against Jews, even though it had been exposed as fraudulent by *The Times* of London as early as 1921.

It was in fact concocted by an ultra-orthodox Christian member of Tsar Nicholas II's secret police, Sergei Nilus, in about 1903. Mark Weitzman and Steven Leonard Jacobs explore the devastating effects of the Protocols in *Dismantling the Big Lie: the Protocols of the Elders of Zion*, stating that 'of all the anti-Jewish screeds, it is the Protocols of the Elders of Zion that emboldens and empowers antisemites. While other antisemitic works may have a sharper intellectual base, it is the conspiratorial imagery of the Protocols that has fuelled the imagination and hatred of Jews and Judaism, from the captains of industry like Henry Ford, to teenage Hamas homicide bombers.'[18]

We see the Protocols reappearing both on the far right and in the Muslim world, and it is picked up online too in some of the increasingly common vicious attacks about Jewish conspiracies that appear on the left as well. The very use of the Protocols, giving that fake work any credence at all, is antisemitic in itself.

Antisemitism in the Modern Muslim World

It wasn't until the failure of Arab nationalism in the late 1970s that Islamist antisemitism really took off. The founding charter of Hamas refers approvingly to the Protocols. And the leader of the 1979 Iranian Revolution, Ayatollah Khomeini, declared in his 1970 book *Islamic Government* that 'Jews and their foreign backers are opposed to the very foundations of Islam and wish to establish Jewish domination throughout the world.' Khomeini's successor, Ayatollah Khamenei, often denies the Holocaust, and he and other Iranian leaders routinely refer to the global dominance of 'Jewish' and 'Zionist' forces – terms that they use interchangeably.

Elsewhere, Iran's Shia proxy, Hezbollah, has fought to keep Anne Frank's diary out of Lebanese schools as part of a Holocaust denial campaign. Its leader, Hasan Nasrallah, has been credited with many antisemitic and Holocaust denying remarks, but is also famous for arguing that if all the Jews were to gather in Israel, Hezbollah would not need to pursue them around the world, presumably in order to destroy them.[19]

Explicit antisemitism is now commonplace in Middle Eastern political discourse. And much of it is being re-imported into Europe, where it started, and, sadly, it can now be found among some impoverished and disaffected Muslim immigrant communities.[20]

For his Channel 4 film *Blaming the Jews*, David Aaronovitch went to meet the Hamas leader Abdelaziz al-Rantisi. He asked him why, in article 32 of the Hamas covenant, there was an approving reference to the Protocols of the Elders of Zion and why the Hamas covenant should argue that 'the Zionists' want an Israel that extends from Cairo to Basra with the next stop being the world.

Asked how he could possibly give any adherence to what is generally agreed to be a fake, Rantisi answered: 'I didn't want to believe it, but then I saw what was happening in Palestine, and I could see that it was genuine.' That was his answer. It was also Hitler's answer. In *Mein Kampf*, the future Führer allowed that many people thought that the Protocols were a forgery, but that he was sure they embodied the truth. 'The best criticism applied to them,' he said, 'is reality.'[21]

Aaronovitch points to the huge amount of antisemitic discourse – in literature and on TV – in Arab countries. Since his film aired back in 2003, social media has taken over in spewing out the hatred. It is undeniably there. But the oddest thing, which Aaronovitch points out, is how those journalists and politicians in parts of the Middle East have taken over 'the ancient political sewers of old Europe for arguments.' He goes on to ask 'what on earth is the blood libel doing in a column in the respected Egyptian mass daily paper *Al-Ahram*, in a book by the Syrian defence minister and in broadcast sermons from various Palestinian mosques?'

Aaronovitch is right to point out the way the political nature of modern Muslim antisemitism has picked up on old Christian antisemitic tropes. As he says, in the nineteenth century, the religious antisemitism of the Christian world turned into a racial antisemitism – if indeed, as we discuss later, Jews can be described as a race. Some rulers and journalists in Muslim countries have picked this up and somehow perverted it into a political and racial view

– even though Muslims and Jews are so alike in many different ways.

So there is a relatively modern strain of antisemitism to be found among some Muslim organisations, and far more among Islamists. It is clear, too, that organisations such as Hamas and Hezbollah are riddled with it. To what extent this is 'political' and to what extent 'religious' is a false dichotomy. It would be perfectly possible to abhor Israel's actions and dislike its presence in the Middle East without falling into what are the originally Christian antisemitic tropes of the Protocols of the Elders of Zion and other appalling antisemitic canards.

Nor is it only in the Middle East. Another classic example comes from Mahathir Mohamad, Malaysia's Prime Minister, who argues that the term antisemitism was invented to stop people from criticising Jews, making them the only race that is beyond reproach.

'There is one race that cannot be criticized,' he said in an interview with the Associated Press. 'If you are anti-Semitic, it seems almost as if you are a criminal . . . anti-Semitic is a term that is invented to prevent people from criticising the Jews for doing wrong things.'[22]

He wrote on his personal blog in 2012 that 'Jews rule this world by proxy.' In 2013, he appeared to urge wiping out all Jews at the Organization of the Islamic Conference summit in Kuala Lumpur:

> There must be a way. And we can only find a way if we stop to think, to assess our weaknesses and our strength, to plan, to strategize and then to counterattack. We are actually very strong. 1.3 billion people cannot be simply wiped out. The Europeans killed six million Jews out of 12 million.

But it is a mixture of classic antisemitic tropes and op-position to the very existence of the State of Israel that defines Malaysia's leader. For Malaysia also decided to ban Israeli competitors from the World Paralympic Swimming Championships in 2019, which led to it being stripped of hosting the competition.[23]

No doubt, then, that in some sections of the Muslim world, a new form of antisemitism has taken hold. And the nature of it, harking back to medieval Christian an-tisemitic tropes, is deeply worrying. It must be legitimate for Muslim leaders, or anyone else for that matter, to be able to criticise Israeli policies or the Israeli government, without falling into this kind of abuse, and without this kind of arrant antisemitism.

But broad stigmatisation of all Muslims as antisemitic is neither accurate not helpful – for while there are heightened levels of both antisemitic and anti-Israel ideas to be found within some Muslim populations, it is also the case that significant proportions of Muslims reject all such prejudice. And non-religious Muslims show the same levels of antisemitism as the wider population. It is clear, too, that many Muslims and Muslim organisations take a different view, show solidarity with Jews when there is an antisemitic attack, as Jews do with Muslims, and use different language. Yet reading Mehdi Hassan on the subject, there is a sorry tale to be found:

If tomorrow, God forbid, I were to cause the death of an innocent man with my car, minutes after sending a series of texts on my mobile phone, I'm guessing I'd spend the rest of my life riddled with guilt. What I wouldn't do is go on television and lay the blame for my subsequent

12-week imprisonment at the door of . . . wait for it . . . the Jews. Yet that's what the Labour peer Nazir Ahmed did in April 2012 . . . He is not a latter-day Goebbels. But herein lies the problem. There are thousands of Lord Ahmeds out there: mild-mannered and well-integrated British Muslims who nevertheless harbour deeply anti-Semitic views . . . the ongoing Israel-Palestine conflict hasn't helped matters. But this goes beyond the Middle East . . . It is sheer hypocrisy for Muslims to complain of Islamophobia in every nook and cranny of British public life, to denounce the newspapers for running Muslim-baiting headlines, and yet ignore the rampant anti-Semitism in our own backyard. We cannot credibly fight Islamophobia while making excuses for Judaeopho-bia . . . we're not all anti-Semites. But, as a community, we do have a 'Jewish problem'.[24]

Modern Antisemitism in Europe: The Nineteenth Century

Modern antisemitism really started to gather force as a political force, different from the old religious hatred, in 1879, when the German journalist Wilhelm Marr pub-lished a pamphlet entitled *Der Sieg des Judenthums über das Germanenthum. Vom nicht confessionellen Standpunkt aus betrachtet* – 'The Victory of the Jewish Spirit over the Germanic Spirit. Observed from a non-religious perspec-tive.' He used *Semitismus* 'Semitism' interchangeably with the word *Judentum* 'Judaism or Jewry', to describe both the Jews as a collective and 'Jewishness' – some sense of the quality of being Jewish.

Marr was married three times; his first two wives

were Jewish, and his third wife was the product of a Christian-Jewish marriage. All of which suggests Marr knew Jews and lived among them – and yet he was a virulent antisemite.

As an elected member of the Hamburg Parliament, he had attacked the elected liberal speaker of the house, the Jewish lawyer Isaac Wolffson, accusing him and other Jews of betraying the democratic movement and abusing their emancipation – their final freeing from legal restrictions that had been placed on Jews from the Middle Ages until the nineteenth century – in order to enter the city's merchant class. There were extensive public protests, and Marr failed to be re-elected.

Marr's view was that assimilation did not help Jews to become 'proper' Germans and that, instead, Germans and Jews were locked in a longstanding conflict, the origins of which he attributed to race. In his view, the Jews were winning; he believed that, through emancipation, Jews had been allowed to gain control of German finance and industry – an accusation we still see cropping up all too often on social media. And, since this conflict was due to 'the essential differences between the Jewish and German races', nothing – even total assimilation of the Jewish population, even if they all became Christian – could solve it other than with the victory of one and the ultimate death of the other. How prescient.

Marr went on to found the *Antisemiten-Liga*, League of Antisemites, the first German organisation committed to combating the alleged threat to Germany and German culture posed by the Jews and their influence, and advocating their forced removal from the country. His ideas became very popular, were published and republished widely, and were shared by many influential politicians and academics.

Heinrich von Treitschke, a Prussian nationalist historian, was one of the few important public figures who supported the antisemitic attacks that became prevalent from 1879 onwards and shared many of Marr's views. Like Marr, he believed Jews were essentially different; he accused them of refusing to assimilate into German culture and society, and denied they played any useful role at all. His thinking gives a clear example of what marks out antisemitism from other forms of racism – that Jews are to blame for everything, and are simultaneously alien, useless *and* too powerful. It stinks of a conspiracy theory. Von Treitschke also coined the expression *Die Juden sind unser Unglück*, 'the Jews are our misfortune', which, decades later, was used in Nazi propaganda.

It was also in the late nineteenth century that the term antisemitism came about. The first known use of *antisemitisch* dates back to 1880 when the Austrian Jewish scholar Moritz Steinschneider attacked the French philosopher Ernest Renan's ideas about how 'Semitic races' were inferior to 'Aryan races'.

Until that point, Semitic was a term used to describe languages of the Semitic group – Arabic, Hebrew, Akkadian, Assyrian, Aramaic, and so on. But from the outset, the term antisemitism did not encompass all speakers of Semitic languages, but only referred to prejudice against Jews, most of whom, at that late nineteenth-century point in history, may have prayed in Hebrew but certainly could not speak it.

The term itself is a strange one, given that while Semitic languages exist, 'Semitism' does not. It is spelled variously with and without a hyphen, with modern opinion favouring no hyphen to make it clear that you can't be anti-Semitic because Semitism, to which you are opposed, does not exist.

Indeed, many scholars were so horrified at the time about the misuse of the terms Semite and Semitic that they invented a new term, Judeophobia, attributed to Leon (Judah Leib) Pinsker and his anonymously published 1882 pamphlet *Autoemancipation*, subtitled *Mahnruf an seine Stammesgenossen, von einem russischen Juden* – 'Warning to His Fellow People, from a Russian Jew'. Pinsker described Judeophobia as an irrational fear or hatred of Jews, which he believed was an inherited characteristic: 'to the living the Jew is a corpse, to the native a foreigner . . . for all a hated rival.'

However, despite his best efforts, and those of his contemporaries, the term antisemitism, or anti-Semitism, stuck and antisemitic ideas grew apace.

The Jewish 'Race'

Throughout the late nineteenth and first half of the twentieth centuries, racial theory and eugenics were fashionable. Anthropologists, in their relatively new science, taught that race was an entirely biological phenomenon and that this was core to a person's behaviour and identity, a position commonly called racial essentialism, which led to so-called 'scientific racism'. Theorists such as Georges Vacher de Lapouge (1854–1936), the founder of so-called socioanthropology, became popular and influential. In 1899, he published *L'Aryen et son rôle social*, 'The Aryan and his social role', in which he classified humanity into various, hierarchised races, using cranial measurements as part of his research. The Jews, with their short skulls, were categorised as those who were destined to be ruled over by stronger races. He saw Jews as having some similarities to the Aryans, but it was for exactly this reason he considered them to be particularly dangerous. They were the only group threatening to displace the Aryan aristocracy.

Vacher de Lapouge went on to become one of the leading sources of Nazi antisemitism and Nazi racist ideology. His work, and that of others, made anti-Jewish prejudice a 'scientific' matter – it wasn't just opinion, it was grounded in fact. Jews were stigmatised: they were thought to have male menstruation, pathological hysteria and nymphomania, all of which sounds absurd now, but these theories were so prevalent that they even began to convince Jews themselves. Several prominent Jewish scholars, notably Joseph Jacobs and Samuel Weissenberg, endorsed these pseudoscientific theories, convinced that the Jews formed a distinct race.[25]

After the Nazi eugenics programme, it is hardly surprising that racial essentialism went out of favour. A significant number of modern anthropologists and biologists in the West came to view race as an invalid genetic or biological designation for people at all. Although some anthropologists still try to categorise using a variety of distinctive traits, most now argue that, among human beings, race has no taxonomic significance. All living human beings belong to the same species, *Homo sapiens*. So Jews cannot be a race, whatever else we might be.

It is worth pausing here to consider just what Jews are, if not a race.

Jews are to some extent a 'people', but not a nation in the sense of a nation state; Jews may or may not share ethnicity, given that Ashkenazi Jews may have more genetic features in common with the people among whom they live than with Sephardi Jews, and vice versa. Jews are bound by the Jewish faith, except by no means all Jews believe or practise that faith. And Jews are often people who were born into Jewish, or partly Jewish, families, irrespective of belief. Jews can also be people who have formally converted to Judaism, who do not share the historic, ancestral links those born into Jewish families possess. And, although most Jews do not accept them as such, since the late nineteenth century antisemites have tended to classify as Jewish those whose ancestors were Jewish, on the basis of the discredited 'racial' argument, rather than a religious definition. That was the case even if their great grandparents had converted to Christianity long before. And Jews themselves have traditionally regarded as Jews those born to Jewish mothers, not fathers, though in some sections of the Jewish community that has changed, and a Jew is now the child of at least one Jewish parent, whether mother or father being immaterial.

What most Jews do share, however, is a sense of peoplehood. The relevant Hebrew word here is *amm* – *amm Yisrael chai*, 'The people of Israel lives', with Israel as a term for the group rather than the state. Its close relative is the Arabic word *ummah*, meaning 'people' or 'community' (*amm* and *ummah* have both senses), which Muslims use to describe a sense of shared peoplehood with other Muslims, although the precise nature of views of peoplehood between Jews and Muslims differs markedly.

So we may feel we are part of a people. But throughout

history it has been others who have chosen how to define Jews, and, by extension, antisemitism.

From the Christian anti-Judaism of the Middle Ages to the pseudo-scientific racial stereotyping of the nineteenth century, to the Nazis' wholehearted adoption of the pseudo-science combined with a vicious hatred, the people who define Jews and Jew hatred have varied and changed.

In recent times, it has been increasingly considered that it is up to the victims of racism – at least to some extent – to describe its nature and characteristics; that those who experience it need to define it. Much of that view is derived, in the UK, from the Macpherson report in which a racist incident was defined as: 'any incident which is perceived to be racist by the victim or any other person.'[26]

If one took that view to its natural conclusion, only the victims of racist attacks can decide whether or not an attack is racist. But that clearly will not do. Nor is it what is really argued in the Macpherson report. What is being said is that the targets, the victims, can define how it feels, and can say whether a specific incident is racist or not, from how they experienced it. But that does not mean that only black people can define racism against black people, only Muslims define Islamophobia or Jews antisemitism. In the case of Stephen Lawrence, and the Macpherson report, the need to define a racist incident was not lexicographical but operational. The importance of classification in that case was that it would determine how the police treated what happened. By previously putting little weight on the views of the victim, and exclusive weight on the views of a possibly prejudiced and ignorant police officer, the police could systematically ignore the rise of attacks that were racist in origin. As antisemitic incidents rise in the UK, there might need to be a similar operational definition of antisemitism. And that is at least in part why a more generally agreed definition was deemed necessary at the beginning of this millennium.

Antisemitism in Pre-War and Wartime Germany

Martin Luther, the passionate antisemite, had assumed that Jews would eventually abandon Judaism and accept conversion to his reformist Christianity. When they failed to do so, Luther's venom went unmatched until 400 years later when Hitler sought to fulfil Luther's instructions.

For it was not very long ago that most of the mainstream churches in Germany (with the honourable exception of the Confessing Church) supported the Hitler regime and were suffused with virulent antisemitism. It was not such a difficult leap for them to make, given this long history of Christian anti-Judaism.

Some of the ideas to be found in Nazi antisemitism had their roots in particular historical aspects of Christian thought. Purity of the blood became a key part of Nazi ideology, and may have had its roots in a doctrine that originated in fifteenth-century Catholic Spain. That doctrine stated that the unfaithfulness of the *deicide* Jews had not only endured in those who converted to Catholicism but had also been transmitted by blood to their descendants, regardless of their sincerity in professing the Christian faith. As a result, Old Christians 'of pure blood' considered New Christians (converts) impure and therefore inadequate members of their communities.

Jews, even if they converted to Christianity, could not win!

Centuries later, these laws were adopted by the Nazis to legitimise their racist, murderous regime. Jews were no longer just objects of fear, but of disgust – they were impure. By 1938, in the aftermath of the appalling attacks on Jewish-owned businesses, synagogues and people on Kristallnacht, Joseph Goebbels, the minister for propaganda in the Nazi regime, was able to declare that 'The German people is anti-Semitic. It has no desire to have its rights restricted or to be provoked in the future by parasites of the Jewish race.'[27] Thanks to a late nineteenth-century construct, in Hitler's Europe, 'Jew' was a term of abuse.

Some scholars have argued that the New Testament itself contributed toward subsequent antisemitism in the Christian community. The theologian A. Roy Eckardt has asserted that the foundation of antisemitism and responsibility for the Holocaust lies ultimately in the New Testament, insisting that Christian repentance must include a re-examination of basic theological attitudes toward Jews and the New Testament in order to deal effectively with antisemitism.[28]

Antisemitism on the Far–Right: White Supremacy, White Nationalism and Racism Reborn

White supremacy has ideological foundations that date back to the so-called scientific racism discussed above (p. 28). It argues that white Europeans are superior to those from other races – if those races exist at all – and are superior to Jews. In the United States, home of much of this type of thinking, the denial of social and political freedom to minorities continued well into the mid-twentieth century, ultimately leading to the Civil Rights movement. It took until 1967 for the Supreme Court to rule against state bans on interracial marriage. And it was only after this that widespread belief in white racial superiority became a minority view.

But it was not a minority view everywhere, or with everyone. White supremacy remains an important ideology to the American far-right, and it has its echoes in the UK's National Front, British National Party, English Defence League and others. Violent right-wing movements are still to be found in the United States, notably the Ku Klux Klan, along with neo-Nazi organisations. Jews and others worldwide were shocked by the Charlottesville rally, a white supremacist rally held in August 2017. Those attending were members of the far-right and included self-identified members of the alt-right, neo-fascists, white nationalists, neo-Nazis, and Klansmen. They chanted racist and antisemitic slogans, carried semi-automatic rifles, Nazi and neo-Nazi symbols, plus other symbols of various past and present anti-Muslim and antisemitic groups. The event turned violent after protesters clashed with counter-protesters, leaving more than thirty injured. Nearby, self-identified white supremacist James Alex Fields Jr. deliberately rammed his car into a crowd of counter-protesters, killing Heather Heyer and injuring nearly forty other people. It was at that rally that marchers were heard shouting, among other things, that 'Jews will not replace us'.[29]

After this, President Donald Trump did not denounce the marchers explicitly, instead condemning 'hatred, bigotry, and violence on many sides', and referring to 'very fine people on both sides', which was interpreted as implying moral equivalence between the white supremacist marchers and those who protested against them.

There is no doubt that the arrival of social media has made it easier to get these ideas widely circulated again. Regular channels such as Twitter, YouTube and Facebook have been part of this, leading to calls for regulation if self-regulation does not control the hate, while platforms such as Stormfront, an alt-right portal for white supremacists with similar beliefs, Gab, 4chan and Reddit have allowed the further spread of white nationalism. And tracking Twitter and some of the hatred to be found on it makes it clear that spreading hate has not only become much easier in recent years, but it has also become infinitely more anonymous, so safer for its perpetrators.

But some is not anonymous, and among the most worrying is the association of the far-right activist and convicted fraudster Tommy Robinson (real name Stephen Yaxley-Lennon) with the UK Independence Party (UKIP), where he has served as a political adviser to its leader, Gerard Batten, since November 2018. Robinson was a co-founder, former spokesman and former leader of the English Defence League (EDL) organisation, a member of the British National Party (BNP), and briefly joint vice-chairman of the British Freedom Party (BFP). He also became involved with the development of Pegida UK in 2015, a British chapter of the German-based Pegida organisation (Patriotic Europeans Against the Islamisation of the West). And he has made frequent appearances on online videos for The Rebel Media, a Canadian far-right political website.

Though Robinson denies racism and antisemitism, many of the EDL's members were people who described themselves as anti-Muslim. To add to that, in 2018 he attended court in support of Mark Meechan, who had been charged for a hate crime after posting footage online of a dog performing Nazi salutes in response to the phrases 'gas the Jews' and 'Sieg Heil'. Meechan was found guilty because the video was 'antisemitic and racist in nature' and was aggravated by religious prejudice. Though Robinson eventually left the EDL, after release from prison in 2015 he returned to anti-Islam demonstrations with Pegida UK.

He was permanently banned from Twitter for violating its rules on 'hateful conduct', and, in February 2019, he was banned by Facebook and YouTube for violating community standards and 'posting material that uses dehumanizing language and calls for violence targeted at Muslims'. But this was only after, among other things, he had falsely accused a Syrian refugee boy, mercilessly bullied at school, of having attacked two schoolgirls, leading to intimidation and violence so serious that the family had to relocate.

Meanwhile, Robinson has attracted sympathy from several right-wing politicians in Europe, including the Dutch Party for Freedom leader Geert Wilders. Yet Robinson, with his extreme anti-Muslim and antisemitic views, and a convicted fraudster, is now an adviser to the UKIP leader, despite many prominent UKIP members, including eight of its MEPs, resigning from the party in response to his appointment.

Open intolerance on the right of the political spectrum has been considered part of the underbelly of

British society for a long time, but its recent resurgence should arouse widespread concern. Tensions around the decision to leave the EU seem to have made it easier for the haters to express their hatred. After the Brexit vote, anti-immigrant feeling was openly displayed – 'Poles, go home' was to be seen on billboards in parts of East Anglia. Xenophobia, always an undercurrent in most societies, was no longer something secretive. The far-right is gaining ground and, as the Brexit debate continues over months and years, this thinking, which includes Islamophobia and antisemitism, may become more central in UK politics – a source of shame, anger and, for Jews, worry for the future.

Defining Antisemitism

The Oxford English Dictionary defines antisemitism as 'hostility to or prejudice against Jews'. As a very basic definition, it is fine. But it does not help us when it comes to understanding antisemitism in all its many and varied forms.

Antisemitism can masquerade as anti-Zionism. It can be associated with claims that Jews are too powerful, or too rich – part of the capitalist oppressor class. Antisemitism can go hand in hand with a set of conspiracy theories. It can form an element of the anti-elite thinking sweeping much of the Western world. And increasingly the calling out of antisemitism is seen as being 'weaponised', used – unfairly, by those who argue this – to discredit those against whom the complaints of antisemitic behaviours or attitudes are made, and nothing to do with genuine antisemitic feeling. As a result of this confusion, a variation on an age-old theme, we began to need something much more detailed, a definition that takes into account the years of persecution that Jews have suffered and the lies and myths that have waxed and waned, but never disappear completely. When it became clear that old antisemitic tropes were being used widely, and revised but never rejected, a new definition was clearly called for.

In recent years, the International Holocaust Remembrance Alliance (IHRA), an intergovernmental organisation that brings together governments and experts to strengthen, advance and promote Holocaust education, research and remembrance worldwide, produced a definition of antisemitism. That definition has become widely accepted. A total of 31 countries have adopted it, as well as more than 130 local councils in the UK, the police, the Crown Prosecution Service and the judiciary.

The founding document of the IHRA is the Declaration of the Stockholm International Forum on the Holocaust (or 'Stockholm Declaration').[30] Part of the Stockholm Declaration states:

> With humanity still scarred by ... antisemitism and xenophobia the international community shares a solemn responsibility to fight those evils.

This was in response to rising antisemitic discourse, and several attacks on Jewish schools and buildings in the late 1990s.

The IHRA definition is itself an offshoot of one created in 2005 by the European Union's Monitoring Centre for Racism and Xenophobia, in those days the EU's leading anti-racism body. It is worth looking closely at what it says.

Antisemitism is a certain perception of Jews, which may be expressed as hatred toward Jews. Rhetorical and physical manifestations of antisemitism are directed toward Jewish or non-Jewish individuals and/or their property, toward Jewish community institutions and religious facilities.

The IHRA's own definition specifies eleven 'contemporary examples of antisemitism', while making it clear that there may be others. These are:

Calling for, aiding, or justifying the killing or harming of Jews in the name of a radical ideology or an extremist view of religion.

Making mendacious, dehumanising, demonising, or stereotypical allegations about Jews as such or the power of Jews as collective – such as, especially but not exclusively, the myth about a world Jewish conspiracy or of Jews controlling the media, economy, government or other societal institutions.

Accusing Jews as a people of being responsible for real or imagined wrongdoing committed by a single Jewish person or group, or even for acts committed by non-Jews.

[　]

Denying the fact, scope, mechanisms (e.g. gas chambers) or intentionality of the genocide of the Jewish people at the hands of National Socialist Germany and its supporters and accomplices during World War II (the Holocaust).

Accusing the Jews as a people, or Israel as a state, of inventing or exaggerating the Holocaust.

[　]

Accusing Jewish citizens of being more loyal to Israel, or to the alleged priorities of Jews worldwide, than to the interests of their own nations.

Denying the Jewish people their right to self-determination, e.g. by claiming that the existence of a State of Israel is a racist endeavour.

[ ]

Applying double standards by requiring of it a behaviour not expected or demanded of any other democratic nation.

[ ]

Using the symbols and images associated with classic antisemitism (e.g. claims of Jews being responsible for killing Jesus or the blood libel) to characterise Israel or Israelis.

[ ]

Drawing comparisons of contemporary Israeli policy to that of the Nazis.

[ ]

Holding Jews collectively responsible for actions of the State of Israel. Manifestations might include the targeting of the State of Israel, conceived as a Jewish collectivity. However, criticism of Israel similar to that levelled against any other country cannot be regarded as antisemitic. Antisemitism frequently charges Jews with conspiring to harm humanity, and it is often used to blame Jews for 'why things go wrong.' It is expressed in speech, writing, visual forms and action, and employs sinister stereotypes and negative character traits.

Some countries or institutions that have failed to sign up have done so because of one or other of these examples.

The truth is that the IHRA definition is not perfect. Sometimes it does not go far enough, and sometimes it is not entirely clear. There is, even now, no foolproof definition of antisemitism.[31] But it is the best we have.

Even though the IHRA definition is now commonly accepted, it is worth remembering what the great historian Walter Laqueur, himself a teenage refugee from Nazi persecution, who commented frequently on the subject, said about defining antisemitism:

> Jews will be under pressure and attack in many parts of the world mainly (but not entirely) because of their insistence that they have rights not only as individuals but also as a national group . . . Whether to call this pressure antisemitism or Judeophobia or post-racialist antisemitism or radical anti-Zionism is a fascinating semantic question that can be endlessly discussed . . . But whatever terminology is used, there is no reason to believe that the last chapter in the long history of antisemitism has already been written.[32]

Walter Laqueur was no innocent. He saw antisemitism morph into new forms, and he knew it could have many names. But it was still the same age-old hatred, dressed up in new clothes. Laqueur died in September 2018, his life having spanned almost a century. He saw the worst that antisemitism can lead to, and he saw the world revolt against it. But he also knew that antisemitism would raise its ugly head again and again, and he knew that coming to a precise definition was difficult, but that we must at least try.

CHAPTER 2

What it is – and what it isn't

The history of antisemitism, as we have seen, is long and fraught. It was firmly embedded in the Christian psyche long before it was perverted by Nazi ideology. Many of the old ideas, even if not consciously believed, still make their way into some modern antisemitism, and that is why it is worth looking at what is, and what isn't, antisemitic in our day. And those ideas range from criticism of the State of Israel in extreme terms – what one might call vilification rather than criticism – to viewing Jews as filthy capitalists, associating them with money, ostentation and power. They range from the antisemitism to be found in the Muslim world – partly, but not wholly, related to the problems of the Middle East – to the often cited canard that Jews control the media. They do not. And there are many more, from conspiracy theories to disgust, from envy to sheer lies.

Criticism of Israel

'But surely you don't believe,' it is frequently put to me, 'that *all* criticism of Israel is antisemitic?' It is a patronising question, of course, in that it is obviously phrased so that all civilised, right-minded people would answer 'no' or 'of course not'.

Whether criticism of Israel and Zionism is in itself antisemitic, or the extent to which it is or is not antisemitic, is a thoroughly vexed area in public discourse. Israel and Zionism have always been the subject of contention and criticism – both from outside the Jewish community and from within it.[1] And much of the criticism of Israel does not stem in any way from antisemitism. But, and it's an important 'but', there is a substantial and growing antisemitic component in the criticism which has been manifesting itself more and more frequently in the spreading of stories that are simply untrue, by ignoring evidence and by drawing conclusions that are wilfully unbalanced. It is why concern has grown within the Jewish community when we hear 'I'm not an antisemite; I'm just an anti-Zionist.' What does that really mean? Does it mean Jews, alone of all peoples, have no right to self-determination? Does it mean that the idea of a 'Jewish homeland' is misconceived? Does it mean all Jews should be blamed for any action of the State of Israel? Does it mean all Jews must have divided loyalties, and one can't trust their patriotism? Or is it a combination of these questions and others that preoccupy the so-called 'anti-Zionists'?

Before we look at mainstream views on Zionism and indeed Israel within the UK, we need to understand the history. During the late nineteenth and early twentieth centuries, the Russian Empire contained the majority of the world's Jews living within its borders. Most of them lived within the so-called Pale of Settlement, a region of Imperial Russia with varying borders that existed from 1791 to 1917, in which permanent residency by Jews was allowed and beyond which Jewish residency was mostly forbidden, other than for those with university education, and a few others. According to a Russian census of 1897, the total Jewish population of Russia was over five million people.

From the late eighteenth century, there was a considerable drive for emancipation, integration and secular education among the Russian Jewish population. The tsars' response to increasing unrest among the Jews was to impose tight quotas on Jewish access – the so-called *numerus clausus* – to schools, universities and cities. Added to that, from 1827 to 1917, many Russian Jewish boys were forced to serve in the Russian army for twenty-five years, starting from the age of twelve – an attempt to destroy their ethnic identity.

It is often alleged that Konstantin Pobedonostsev, chief adviser under three tsars, had said that one-third of Russia's Jews was expected to emigrate, one-third to accept baptism, and one-third to starve.[2] True or not, his antisemitic views are clear from what he is known to have said to the British author Arnold White:

> The characteristics of the Jewish race are parasitic; for their sustenance they require the presence of another race as 'host' although they remain aloof and self-contained. Take them from the living organism, put them on a rock, and they die. They cannot cultivate the soil.[3]

There were many terrible antisemitic incidents in nineteenth-century Russia. But it was the Kishinev pogrom of 1903 that finally prompted many Jews to leave. Between 1880 and 1928, two million Jews emigrated, mostly to the United States, though some came to the UK (sometimes mistakenly, sometimes because they

could not afford the fare as far as the US); a minority
chose Palestine. That was because there had already been
discussions about self-determination for the Jews half a
century earlier. Moses Hess, once an associate of Karl
Marx and Friedrich Engels, wrote *Rome and Jerusalem* in
1862, in which he called for the Jews to create a socialist state in Palestine as a means of settling 'the Jewish
question'.[4] Then, in 1882, after the Odessa pogrom, Leon
Pinsker published the pamphlet *Autoemancipation* ('Self-
emancipation'), in which he argued that Jews could only
be truly free if they could live in their own country. He
analysed the persistent tendency of Europeans to regard
Jews as aliens:

> Since the Jew is nowhere at home, nowhere regarded as a
> native, he remains an alien everywhere. That he himself
> and his ancestors as well are born in the country does not
> alter this fact in the least.[5]

The desire for Jews to settle in Palestine had remarkable
support from many British Protestant clergy and others.
They were arguing strongly for 'restorationism' (the restoration of Jews to the Holy Land as a fulfilment of Biblical
prophecy) long before Jewish Zionists were really active.
Take, for instance, Charles Spurgeon, the Baptist nick-
named the 'Prince of Preachers', who said in a sermon
as early as 1864, written for the British Society for the
Propagation of the Gospel among the Jews:

> The meaning of our text, as opened up by the context, is
> most evidently, if words mean anything, first, that there
> shall be a political restoration of the Jews to their own
> land and to their own nationality.[6]

These ideas about the restoration of the Jews to their proper status within the Land of Israel became part of British public discourse in the early nineteenth century, as part of the British Protestant revival. Lord Shaftesbury's 'Memorandum to Protestant Monarchs of Europe for the restoration of the Jews to Palestine', published in the *Colonial Times* in 1841, is a perfect case in point. As a result of his lobbying, Britain had established a consulate in Jerusalem in 1838, the first diplomatic appointment in the city. Disraeli shared these views. He then planned to restore the nation to Palestine, his real ambition, as he wrote in a letter of 1851: '*Coningsby* [the title of Disraeli's political novel, published in 1844] was merely a feeler – my views were not fully developed at that time – since then all I have written has been for one purpose. The man who should restore the Hebrew race to their country would be the Messiah – the real saviour of prophecy!'[7]

Twenty-six years later, Disraeli wrote in *The Jewish Question is the Oriental Quest* (1877) that, within fifty years, a nation of one million Jews would reside in Palestine under the guidance of the British.[8]

But it was the Dreyfus Affair, which erupted in 1894, that had the greatest effect of all in making many Jews – and a considerable number of sympathetic non-Jews – feel that the Jews needed their own nation state, a homeland. It was a political scandal that rocked the Third French Republic from 1894 to 1906. Captain Alfred Dreyfus, a young French artillery officer of Jewish descent, was sentenced to life imprisonment in 1894 for allegedly communicating French military secrets to the German Embassy in Paris. Yet there was clear evidence that identified a French Army major, Ferdinand Esterhazy, as the real culprit. High-ranking military officials suppressed that evidence, and Esterhazy was acquitted. The Army then brought more charges against Dreyfus, based on falsified documents. When Émile Zola, a well-known French writer, learned of the military court's framing of Dreyfus and of an attempted cover-up, he wrote *J'Accuse . . .!*, a vehement open letter published in 1898.[9] In 1899, Dreyfus was retried. French society was by now divided between those who supported Dreyfus, and those who condemned him. Dreyfus was convicted again, but given a pardon and set free. In 1906, Dreyfus was totally exonerated and reinstated as a major in the French Army.

The depth of antisemitism in what had been the first country to grant Jews equal rights led many Jews to question their future prospects in Christian Europe. This was a key moment that changed thinking about Jewish futures in the West. An Austro-Hungarian Jewish journalist, Theodor Herzl, was so moved by what happened that he began to believe that only the creation of a Jewish state would enable the Jews to join the family of nations – and thus escape antisemitism. The irony of that – given present confusion between anti-Zionism and antisemitism, and the one morphing into the other – is hard to deny.

The First Zionist Congress in Basel in 1897 agreed the following programme, declaring that Zionism 'seeks to establish a home for the Jewish people in Palestine secured under public law':

> The promotion by appropriate means of the settlement in Palestine of Jewish farmers, artisans, and manufacturers.
>
> The organisation and uniting of the whole of Jewry by means of appropriate institutions, both local and

international, in accordance with the laws of each country.

The strengthening and fostering of Jewish national sentiment and national consciousness.

Preparatory steps toward obtaining the consent of governments, where necessary, in order to reach the goals of Zionism.

By no means all Jews agreed with this programme. Before the Holocaust, Reform Judaism – a non-orthodox section of the Jewish community, then particularly strong in the United States and Germany – and many assimilated Western European and American Jews, had rejected Zionism as inconsistent with the requirements of Jewish citizenship in the diaspora. The opposition of Reform Judaism was expressed in the Pittsburgh Platform as early as 1885 by the Central Conference of American Rabbis:

> We consider ourselves no longer a nation but a religious community, and therefore expect neither a return to Palestine, nor a sacrificial worship under the administration of the sons of Aaron, nor the restoration of any of the laws concerning the Jewish state.

But the Dreyfus affair changed much of that. Meanwhile, back in the UK, two months after the British declaration of war against the Ottomans, the British, and Jewish, member of the government Herbert Samuel presented a detailed memorandum to the British Cabinet, entitled 'The Future of Palestine', discussing the benefits of a British protectorate over Palestine to support Jewish immigration. At that time, the most prominent

Russian-Jewish-Zionist migrant in Britain was the chemist Chaim Weizmann, later the first President of the State of Israel. Weizmann had developed a new process for producing acetone through bacterial fermentation, what is known as the acetone–butanol–ethanol fermentation process. It was a critical ingredient in manufacturing the kinds of explosives that Britain had – hitherto – been unable to manufacture in sufficient quantities. David Lloyd George became the minister responsible for armaments, and asked Weizmann to develop his process for mass production. Lloyd George was himself an evangelical Christian, and also pro-Zionist. When Lloyd George asked Weizmann about payment for his scientific work that so helped Britain during the war, Weizmann's reply was that he did not want any money, but did want the rights over Palestine. From then on, Weizmann became a close associate of Lloyd George (Prime Minister from 1916) and the then First Lord of the Admiralty (Foreign Secretary from 1916), Arthur Balfour.

However, in August 1917, while the British cabinet was discussing the Balfour Declaration, drafted to Lloyd George's orders after Weizmann's valiant efforts, the staunchly anti-Zionist Edwin Montagu, the only Jew in the British Cabinet at that time, declared himself 'passionately opposed to the declaration'. He argued this on the grounds that '(a) it was a capitulation to anti-Semitic bigotry, with its suggestion that Palestine was the natural destination of the Jews, and that (b) it would be a grave cause of alarm to the Muslim world'.[10] In response, additional sections were added to the declaration, both on the future rights of non-Jews in Palestine and on the status of Jews worldwide. And then, just as the draft was being finalised, the term 'state' was replaced with 'home', and further comments were sought from Zionists abroad. Louis Brandeis, at that time a member of the US Supreme Court, had considerable influence, and he is alleged to have changed the words 'Jewish race' to 'Jewish people'.[11]

On 2 November 1917, the British Foreign Secretary made his landmark Balfour Declaration, publicly expressing the government's view in favour of 'the establishment in Palestine of a national home for the Jewish people', and specifically noting that its establishment must not 'prejudice the civil and religious rights of existing non-Jewish communities in Palestine, or the rights and political status enjoyed by Jews in any other country'. So, after the defeat and dismantling of the Ottoman Empire by the European colonial powers in 1918, the League of Nations endorsed the full text of the Balfour Declaration and established the British Mandate for Palestine.

In 1919, despite considerable Arab opposition, the Hashemite ruler Emir Faisal also signed the Faisal-Weizmann Agreement, an oft-forgotten fact. Faisal wrote:

> We Arabs, especially the educated among us, look with the deepest sympathy on the Zionist movement. Our delegation here in Paris is fully acquainted with the proposals submitted yesterday by the Zionist organization to the Peace Conference, and we regard them as moderate and proper.[12]

Emir Faisal had in fact added a caveat in Arabic next to his signature, stating that he considered the agreement was conditional on Palestine being within the area of

Arab independence. From 1936, there was an Arab uprising, which lasted three years. The Supreme Muslim Council in Palestine, led by the Mufti, organised the revolt. The Mufti was forced to flee to Iraq, where he was involved in a pro-Nazi coup. That led to a pogrom in the Jewish areas of Baghdad. In 1939, he rejected the British White Paper, which had imposed restrictions on Jewish immigration and land acquisition by Jews, just as things in Europe were becoming desperate.

It was the issue of immigration that really divided the Jews and Arabs. Jews saw immigration into what was then Palestine as a way of escaping European persecution, and Arabs could not compromise because to do so would end their majority in the country. Things could only get worse. And, despite the Balfour Declaration and Christian restorationism, British support for Zionism has always been controversial. Churchill restricted Jewish migration into Palestine to an annual quota to be decided by the British. Hitler's rise to power meant increased support among assimilated European Jews for Zionism, and increased pressure to allow Jews fleeing the Nazis into Palestine.

Then in 1939, just as the situation in Germany and Austria was becoming intolerable for the Jews, the British issued a White Paper in which they called for the establishment of a Jewish national home in an independent Palestinian state within ten years, and rejected the idea of partitioning Palestine. 'The independent State should be one in which Arabs and Jews share government in such a way as to ensure that the essential interests of each community are safeguarded.' The White Paper ruled that further Jewish immigration was to be determined by the

Arab majority, since the government believed that further migration into Palestine would be harmful to the Arab population. Because of the horror of what was happening to the Jews of Germany, Austria and the Sudetenland, they relaxed that restriction on any further migration, but only slightly – a further 10,000 Jews a year were to be admitted from 1939 to 1944, plus a one-time allowance of 25,000. The allowance was exceptional, in view of the situation in Europe, and not to be repeated. After that, Jewish migration would require the agreement of the Arab majority (by this time Jews were about one-third of the population).

In 1947, Britain announced its intention to withdraw from Palestine. A United Nations Special Committee investigated the situation and offered two solutions – either to establish a bi-national state in Palestine (the minority option) or to partition Palestine into a Jewish and an Arab state. From the Zionist point of view, the second option corresponded more closely to their ultimate goal, so they gave it full support. On 29 November, the United Nations General Assembly voted to partition Palestine into an Arab state and a Jewish state (with Jerusalem becoming an international enclave). Amid public rejoicing in Jewish communities in Palestine, the Jewish Agency accepted the plan. The Palestinian Arab leadership and the Arab League rejected the decision and announced that they would not abide by it. Civil war between the Arabs and Jews in Palestine ensued, and a lasting peace has never really been achieved. For Palestinians, the Nakba (tragedy or disaster), the 1948 Palestinian exodus, still looms large. More than 700,000 Palestinian Arabs – about half of pre-war Palestine's Arab population – fled, or were expelled from their homes, during the 1948 Palestine war. A series of laws passed by the first Israeli government prevented Arabs who had left from returning to their homes or claiming their property. The status of the refugees, and in particular whether Israel will grant them their claimed right to return to their homes or be compensated, are still key issues in the ongoing Israeli–Palestinian conflict.

Against this background, the State of Israel was established, and has now existed, and prospered in many ways. But there have been many wars. In some, Israel has triumphed. In others, tension and skirmishes remain – with the war in Lebanon and ongoing violence and demonstrations in Gaza a cause of great sadness and anger. And there has been an occupation of the West Bank and Gaza since 1967.

Israel has matured and has become not the socialist dream it once was meant to be, but an increasingly right-wing political entity, with astonishingly impressive hi-tech and healthcare advances, a burgeoning investment economy, and a rich cultural life. Its economic success and its scientific inventiveness are envied worldwide. But it also has battles between religious and secular Jews, troubles around Jerusalem and its status, not to mention who has the right to live there, a hostile Arab world around it, a resentful Palestinian Israeli Arab population, a West Bank occupation that seems never ending and deeply troubled, increasing violence and anger in Gaza, and a government that is increasingly nationalistic and allergic to criticism. And it is partly that shift to the right that has led to greater criticism of Israel by her friends, let alone her enemies.

Questioning the Right of Israel to Exist

Nobody sensible thinks that 'reasonable' criticism of Israel (more on this shortly) is antisemitic; but there is real concern about questioning its right to exist or using explicitly antisemitic language about it, using Zionist, or Zio for short, as a term of abuse, or using vitriolic and vile language about Israel in a way that one would not do about another state.

The argument often comes down to definitions of 'criticism' as much as definitions of 'antisemitism', so it is worth looking at a working definition of what would count as criticism, and what kind of language/activism is designed to argue Israel out of existence, which is where unacceptability lies.

In 2012, the prominent Israeli-American journalist and writer Benjamin Kerstein argued that all criticism of Israel is antisemitic, and that the world increasingly is turned against Israel to the point of willing its destruction:

> A large portion of the world, West and East, has come to believe that Arabs and Muslims have earned the right to murder Jews. Derived from this right, they have also come to believe that the destruction, dismantling, and erasure of the State of Israel, and the slaughter, expulsion, and/or perpetual subjugation of its Jewish population are entirely legitimate and indeed desirable.[13]

Kerstein's argument is that the history of the Jews makes criticism of Israel very dangerous. While he may be over-stating the case, you can see where he is coming from. For Israeli Jews are often convinced the whole world hates them; they feel beleaguered, always confronted with

54

untruths, half-truths and a lack of comparators. Kerstein's argument – that the historical context means Israel should not be criticised at all – clearly does not stand up to any kind of serious analysis. Israel, like any other state, must be prepared to face criticism. But not more than any other state. That's where danger lies, and that's where one could argue there is, or might be, an antisemitic component in play.

Meanwhile, Alexander Zeldin, Senior Communications Associate at the American Jewish Committee, argues that social media is to blame for the growing prevalence of the 'criticising Israel is not antisemitic' argument:

> While Twitter can sometimes enable worthwhile conversations between people who would not otherwise cross paths, it can also function as an echo chamber where the same arguments are repeated ad infinitum. So it is with the usual suspects who constantly feel compelled to assert that 'criticizing Israel isn't anti-Semitic. Calling it anti-Semitic is a silencing tactic.'[14]

Both these writers share the view of many other Jews, that much of the criticism of Israel is motivated by antisemitism. Zeldin picks up on an important point here too – that many critics of Israel argue that defenders try to counter-attack by falsely accusing them of antisemitism. This argument is too simplistic – such a judgement cannot be made without analysing the particular context, tone and accuracy of those criticisms. And I believe that if we are sufficiently clear about what antisemitism is and is not, along with examining the tone of the argument, it should be possible to be clear about whether criticism of

Israel is, or is not, antisemitic. Zeldin argues that the distinction lies in whether the criticism is of Israel's actions or of its existence. On the whole, I agree, but that needs further unpacking:

> Questioning Israel's right to exist or demonizing Zionism, its founding ideology, as uniquely evil is not a 'criticism of Israel.' It's antisemitism masquerading as a political critique. Those who advance this argument are using a well-known racist tactic by, when confronted with their bigotry, responding that their critics are 'playing the race card.' In both cases, it's a strategy of obfuscation designed to enable the continuing assertion of bigoted beliefs without being held responsible for them. In the case of Israel and her supporters, it's also a cheap trick used to sound reasonable while slandering a group – in this case, the Jews.[15]

Denying the State of Israel's right to exist cannot be seen as anything other than antisemitic, because it is denying the Jewish people their right to self-determination – alone of all other peoples. It is arguing that Jews, uniquely, cannot have a country of their own. And, while one might be able to argue legitimately that it would have been possible to be opposed to the creation of the State of Israel before it was established in 1948, for all sorts of reasons, particularly including questions about the rights of Palestinians, it is difficult to argue that it has no right to exist seventy years on, even if one might wish to support the return of the Occupied Territories. What other state would the denier wish to attack in this way, as having no right to exist? There are no campaigns to delegitimise other states, despite plenty of arguments about Jammu/

Kashmir, Macedonia, Catalonia, and others seeking independent, breakaway status.

It is one thing to deny Israel a right to exist at all. But arguing about Israel's borders, or criticising its treatment of its Arab population, or of Palestinians in the Occupied Territories, is another thing entirely. The argument is about policies, not about a right to exist. And though many Israelis, and the Israeli government, would not agree with me in saying this, those are legitimate issues to raise. They are not necessarily antisemitic in intent, unless the level of vitriol in the language and subsequent discussion makes them so.

One of the distinctions one can make between legitimate criticism and antisemitic name-calling is by looking at the extent to which critics examine policies and acknowledge issues such as Israel's security concerns – and accept that both peoples, Palestinians and Israelis, have a right to peace and security. Antisemites, claiming merely to be 'anti-Zionist' critics, tend only to favour the Palestinian cause, and cannot accept that Israelis have just as strong a right to peace and security; nor can they understand, or empathise with, the historical link of Jews to the land of Israel.

Added to that, it must be legitimate to criticise Zionism as a political philosophy – as with any political philosophy, be it socialism or Marxism. It all depends on how it is done. Denying critics their right to debate the philosophy behind Zionism is simply shutting down the argument – always a weak defence.

But things have become more complicated than that. Increasingly, student politics and much hard-left politics have become defined by the BDS movement. BDS stands for Boycott, Divestment and Sanctions, and there is some disagreement over exactly when and how the BDS movement began. The BDS movement's own website suggests that it was on 9 July 2005, on the first anniversary of the advisory opinion by the International Court of Justice in which the West Bank barrier was declared a violation of international law. From then on, it has campaigned for just that – boycotts of Israeli speakers, divestment from any Israeli investment, and sanctions against the State of Israel and its people. Increasingly, BDS advocates criticise Zionism, and use the terms Zionist and Jew interchangeably. It is no longer about a critique of Zionism the political philosophy. In the thinking of the BDS supporters, who often tend to see no historical context, Israel is a racist endeavour, an apartheid state, a colonial oppressor, and guilty of war crimes against the Palestinians. For them, that is the nature of Zionism.

And this is why it needs to be taken head on. There is nothing wrong with arguing that there should be a two state solution to the Israel/Palestine conflict, and that compromise is the best way forward. There's nothing wrong with criticising the long security wall as the Israeli solution to incursion from the Occupied Territories. But there is everything wrong with describing Israel as a racist endeavour (because it is a Jewish state) – that is in itself antisemitic, because no one would argue it is racist to have a state church in the UK or Denmark, or to have Muslim states, governed by a considerable amount of Islamic law, in Saudi Arabia or Iran, to name but two. Why is it racist for Jews, but not for Muslims or Christians?

Equally, to use a boycott to stop speakers who frequently disagree with Israeli government policies from speaking on UK or US university campuses, and to shout them down if they do arrive, is highly questionable. It may not always be antisemitic, but it does suggest an unwillingness to look objectively, an unwillingness to listen to Israel's own opposition spokespeople, and, most worryingly, an attempt to make everything Israeli – its people, its products – toxic, rather than its government. And that could be argued to be antisemitic, if there is no parallel behaviour in relation to any other state and its peoples.

The Nationality Law

I am quite clear that one could argue hard against the BDS movement, and against the accusation that Israel itself is a racist endeavour, and say that such accusations are antisemitic. I think they are. However, the 2018 Israeli Nationality Law, the so-called Basic Law, designed to emphasise the Jewish nature of the state and to lower the status both of non-Jewish citizens and the Arabic language, does not help hold that position, even if it has remarkably little practical effect. It has – understandably, in my view – caused endless ill-feeling in Israel and beyond. Take Abe Silberstein on the subject:

> The law that ultimately passed is an unnecessary and deliberate provocation aimed at Israel's minority groups, especially its Arab citizens ... The law deserves only the disdain of progressive Jews abroad, which it has thankfully garnered in abundance ... However, despite its discriminatory intent, it's important to oppose this law while maintaining unwavering fidelity to the truth,

which is that it says a lot but does very little ... But if we don't need to worry about the implications of this specific law, we should take note of the broader political trends in Israel that brought us to this moment.[16]

I agree. It's the direction of travel, and the fact that it demotes the status of non-Jewish citizens of Israel, that makes it so depressing – and, in my view, morally wrong.

Others defend the law, saying it is up to every state to define its sense of nationhood. The trouble is, if that is to be the case, there is a need for a real explanation of what all this means for Israel's non-Jewish citizens, who now feel that they are – or will be – second-class citizens. After all, it demotes the Arabic language to a 'special status', rather than equal, and for the Druze, who fight in the army and are a key part of Israeli society in all ways, it is a slap in the face.

Most critics, Jews and non-Jews alike, argue the law wasn't needed, because everyone knows Israel is a Jewish state. Israeli Prime Minister Binyamin Netanyahu wanted to enact it to keep in his fragile coalition those right-wing voices who had been trying to get something along its lines through for months, if not years. It is hugely damaging, in a way that Netanyahu chooses not to understand. And it makes it harder for Jews in the diaspora to defend Israel's democracy. It also makes it harder for young diaspora Jews – idealistic about equality and anti-racism, and facing constant arguments, if not vitriol, about Israel on university campuses – to feel sympathy with the State of Israel at all.

I share some of their concerns, despite loving Israel. But equally I see considerable opposition to this kind of thinking within Israel itself – something never mentioned by the anti-Zionists – and a strong NGO presence that challenges all the right-wing moves that have taken place, and especially this new Nationality Law.

Organ Harvesting in Reference to the Blood Libel

But criticism of Israel does not stop at criticising the new nationality legislation. That criticism is entirely legitimate. Some criticism is not – indeed, rather than criticism, it is a perversion of the truth. And arguably antisemitic. Take the suggestion that Israel, often first on the scene with aid, helps in disaster-stricken nations purely in order to harvest organs for Israelis. This horrible accusation originates from something quite different. Back in 2009, Israel admitted that its pathologists had been harvesting skin, corneas, heart valves and bones from the bodies of Palestinians and others, including Israelis, often without permission from relatives – a practice it said had ended in the 1990s.[17]

This followed a furious row prompted by the Swedish newspaper *Aftonbladet* reporting in 2009 that Israel was killing Palestinians in order to use their organs – a charge that Israel denied and called 'antisemitic'. Israel's reaction that this was antisemitic comes from two distinct stands of thought. First, the idea that Jews – and here the Israelis were seeing themselves as Jews – kill people to use their blood or organs for some devious practices has its origins in the Blood Libel discussed above. To that extent it is undoubtedly antisemitic. Second, the accusation that Israelis would be willing to kill Palestinians at all other than in a war setting was desperately upsetting and unfounded. Whether that accusation is necessarily antisemitic rather than merely deeply hostile to Israel, from people willing to believe the (untrue, unevidenced) worst, is a more complicated question.

The *Aftonbladet* story quoted Palestinians as saying young men from the West Bank and Gaza Strip had been seized by the Israeli forces and their bodies returned to their families with missing organs.[18] Israel demanded that Sweden condemn the *Aftonbladet* article, calling it an antisemitic 'blood libel'. Stockholm refused, saying that to do so would violate freedom of speech in the country. The foreign minister then cancelled a visit to Israel.

Despite there being no evidence that Israel had killed anyone for their organs, not to mention the whole accusation's echo of the medieval blood libels, in November 2009, Alison Weir, founder and executive director of the non-profit organisation If Americans Knew (IAK), known for critical views towards Israel, published an article in the *Washington Report on Middle East Affairs* headlined, 'Israeli Organ Trafficking and Theft: From Moldova to Palestine'. In it she stated that 'Israeli organ harvesting – sometimes with Israeli governmental funding and the participation of high Israeli officials, prominent Israeli physicians, and Israeli ministries – has been documented for many years.'[19]

But she is wrong. She also discussed human rights groups in the West Bank complaining of tissue and organs being stolen from slain Palestinians by Israeli pathologists at the national Israeli legal medical institute in Tel Aviv. And she argued that the Israeli Ministry of Defense is heavily implicated in this illicit national 'program' of transplant tourism.[20]

Yet there was and is no evidence of any of this. And so it goes on. Press TV (a news and documentary network affiliated to Islamic Republic of Iran Broadcasting, IRIB) ran a story that Robrecht Vanderbeeken, the cultural secretary of Belgium's ACOD trade union and a philosophy of science scholar, had commented in a column published by Belgian website De Wereld Morgen the previous August, that the population of the Gaza Strip is being 'starved to death, poisoned, and children are kidnapped and murdered for their organs'.[21] Despite complaints, De Wereld Morgen stuck to the assertion that Israel 'kidnapped' and 'murdered' Palestinian children and used organs belonging to the Palestinians its forces killed. Yet there was no evidence for this at all.

All there is, and it is a later story and a disputed one, is a 2014 *New York Times* report that Israelis had played a 'disproportionate role' in organ trafficking since 2000. This has nothing whatever to do with killing anyone for their organs, or even removing them from people already dead. It simply discusses the involvement of some Israelis – and, importantly, not the Israeli government – in transplant tourism.[22]

Organ trafficking is without doubt a vile trade. But it is not the same as killing people in order to harvest their organs. Nevertheless, that does not stop the issue continuing to be raised, including by Baroness Tonge in the UK's House of Lords. In the wake of the *Aftonbladet* article in 2009, she called for Israel to set up an inquiry to disprove allegations that its medical teams in Haiti had 'harvested' organs of earthquake victims for use in transplants. This was when they had gone there to provide emergency relief, and the story had already been strongly rebutted and disproved. The then Liberal Democrat leader Nick Clegg removed her as the party's health spokeswoman in the Lords, describing her remarks as 'wrong, distasteful and provocative'.[23]

The accusation that Israel was harvesting organs in the wake of disaster relief is without doubt an antisemitic slur. But it is important to stress, particularly for people who are not Jewish, the level of distress caused to Jews by this particular canard, because it echoes the age old lie that Jews used the blood of Christian children for ritual purposes.

Freedom of Religion

Another common criticism is that Israel does not allow freedom of religion. According to a 2009 report from the US Department of State's Bureau of Democracy, Human Rights, and Labor,[24] Israel falls short of being a tolerant or pluralistic society and discriminates against Muslims, Jehovah's Witnesses, Reform Jews, Christians, women and Bedouins. To add to that, the 137 official holy sites that are recognised by Israel are all Jewish, ignoring and neglecting Christian and Muslim sites, and leaving them open to decay or the risk of being built on.

The US-based Pew Research Center has also published studies of social hostilities by country. Its Social Hostilities Index (SHI) measures acts of religious hostility by private individuals, organisations or social groups. This includes mob or sectarian violence, harassment over attire for religious reasons and other religion-related intimidation or abuse. In 2007, Israel was one of ten countries with a score over 7.1 on a scale of 10. Furthermore, in 2010,

Israel and the Palestinian territories were two of the fifteen areas with the highest SHI scores.[25]

It is clear that Israel should look to its laurels here. The situation is not good enough – and it cannot be considered antisemitic to point that out. Yet these reports do not capture the full picture – that there is in fact considerable freedom of religion in Israel, though Reform Jews like me, among others, might debate how far it extends. The Bahá'í faith has its headquarters in Haifa, while Christian and Muslim sites receive protection as needed from security forces.

In addition, one of the paradoxical consequences of the recent meltdown in much of the Middle East is that the Christian population of Israel is growing, something rarely commented on by Christian critics of Israel.[26] If it were true that freedom of religion is so limited in Israel, it is unlikely that this particular growth of Christian communities would be occurring. It is clear that there are counter stories, and criticism in this area needs to be carefully evidenced and the nuances in religious tolerance in Israel examined closely.

The Israeli Army

Whenever there is conflict in Israel/Gaza, or when there are rocket strikes into Israel from Gaza or Lebanon, there is always a strong emotional reaction from those who watch what happens. People see the Israeli army acting violently against people throwing stones. They see the Israeli army bulldozing Palestinian houses. They watch the apparently uneven contest and feel distressed. Yet they fail to see the rockets lobbed into Israeli civilian settlements by the Hamas terror group, and they fail to see the level of organisation of young protesters in, say, Gaza, by Hamas leaders. Israel looks huge and powerful and the people of Gaza, sometimes blockaded in, with poor power supplies, look weak and oppressed. Yet it is more complicated than that, for Israel is in fact a small country of nine million people, and the lack of provision of power and other utilities in Gaza is usually more due to Hamas than to the Israelis. None of this is simple.

However, whenever the Israeli army is seen acting defensively, the vitriol in much of the reaction is often expressed almost as hatred of Israel. It is as if Israel is uniquely cruel or tough, as if its forces are uniquely prepared to fight back hard. And when there are demonstrations and stone throwing from young people at the border with Gaza, TV footage can make the Israelis look like the aggressors against unarmed, or poorly armed, civilians. There are undoubtedly times when Israel gets it wrong. Yet however sympathetic one might be to the Palestinian cause, any country is entitled to respond to an attack on its borders, or to an attack from within, even though innocent people will and do get hurt.

But of course Israel's actions against Palestinians can look – and can be – disproportionate. Take for example the sixty-two Gazan Palestinians who were listed by the Hamas-run health ministry in Gaza as having been killed in clashes between tens of thousands of protesters at the border and Israeli troops who were there, guarding the border with Gaza, in May 2018. Israel accused Hamas of encouraging the protests and using them as cover to attempt to carry out terror attacks, while Salah Bardawil, a Hamas spokesperson, claimed fifty out of the sixty-two people listed as killed were members of his organisation. Terrible as it looked to all of us who were watching, it may not have been quite what it seemed. For it may have been more of an organised Hamas raid than a purely civilian demonstration. Whatever the truth, it was appalling to see death rates as high as these, and many people who watched some of what transpired on news coverage were deeply disturbed by what they saw. And it led to a great deal of criticism, much unfair, but some of it fair in the condemnation of the sheer numbers of deaths, and there were questions, in Israel and beyond, as to whether the Israeli forces could have acted with greater restraint.

Censuring Israel

The United Nations has censured Israel more than any other country, many of which commit far worse human rights abuses – Syria, Burma, Sudan, Nepal, Pakistan and many others. Since 2003, the UN has issued 232 resolutions with respect to Israel, 40 per cent of all the resolutions issued by the UN over the period and more than six times that of the second placed country, Sudan.

So why has it been censured so much? Is antisemitism at the bottom of it? For that, we need to examine the issues on which it has been censured.

Settlements in the occupied Palestinian territories is one clear example, and it is certainly the case that many Israelis disapprove of those settlements just as much as critics outside Israel. They also dislike the tone of the 'settlers' on the news, when they appear 'defending' their rights. All too often, they seem to be fundamentalist religious Jews, who lay claim to the 'Biblical lands of Judea and Samaria', which are clearly not wholly part of modern Israel as internationally agreed. They are the original areas of the Biblical northern kingdom of Israel, with its capital in Samaria, and the southern kingdom of Judah. Most Israelis do not refer to them by that name, calling them either the Occupied Territories or the West Bank.

The participating High Contracting Parties to the Fourth Geneva Convention, numerous UN resolutions, the International Court of Justice and others have all ruled that Israel's policy of establishing civilian settlements in territories that are considered to be occupied, including in East Jerusalem, is illegal. Israel disputes the notion that the West Bank and in particular East Jerusalem are occupied under international law, though their view is generally dismissed internationally. But many on the left in Israel also disapprove of the Settlements, and believe that the Israeli government's support for them and defence of them is making any peace moves impossible. The settlements and the occupied territories are why most countries have their embassies in Tel Aviv, not Jerusalem, and why US president Trump's decision to move the American embassy to Jerusalem drew so much fire. He was, de facto, accepting Israel's right to describe Jerusalem – and in that sense all of Jerusalem – as the state capital.

While most people would not deny any country the right to decide upon its own capital, the fact that parts of East Jerusalem are being compulsorily purchased and given to Jewish occupants has raised the tension. Arabs have been displaced, as has happened in the Sheikh Jarrah area, part of East Jerusalem captured by Israel in the 1967 war. The US State Department has called some of this a violation of Israel's obligations under the Roadmap for peace.[27]

Many Israelis on the left see evictions, and the take-over of East Jerusalem, as driving any chance of peace with the Palestinians even further into the future. To add to which, those who are seen as moderate and on the left on these issues in Israel are clear that they would favour displacing the 'settlers' and returning the occupied territories. With peace attempts having stalled, there is no stomach in the Israeli government for further conces-sions. Meanwhile, within those West Bank 'settlements', Jews have the right to vote in Israeli elections – though the territory is 'occupied', and not part of Israel proper – while Arabs living in neighbouring villages do not.

There is much criticism of the lack of parity, both within and outside Israel. I do not believe that criticising Israel for disparity of treatment and rights between Jews and Arabs in the West Bank is antisemitic. Nor do I be-lieve it is antisemitic to criticise Israel for the evictions of Arab families in East Jerusalem. What is, or can be, antisemitic is to do this to the exclusion of criticising any other state with far worse human rights abuses, and to do this in a tone so shrill that rational argument, and under-standing the context, let alone the opposite point of view, is impossible. It is undoubtedly antisemitic to attempt to describe everything about the State of Israel as toxic.

Fair criticism means criticising China for its re-education camps for Muslims in Xinjiang province, which ought to be causing a far greater outcry than they are. Or the treatment of Rohingya Muslims in Burma, or asylum seekers in Sudan, and so on. The important thing here is balance – the willingness to look at human rights abuses worldwide, the willingness to understand that Israel's actions, even its reprehensible ones, are but a tiny element in the litany of appalling acts by government powers, that matters.

So criticism of Israel with no international comparators is unacceptable. BDS without thinking it through, making Israel toxic, is unfair and arguably antisemitic. And those who do it need to ask themselves why. Feeling sorry for the Palestinians and their plight is not enough. Only criticising Israel, never criticising other states, needs close examination. For it is reasonable to argue that people who criticise a Jewish state alone of all others, despite far worse human rights abuses elsewhere, are showing some level of antisemitism.

The Treatment of Palestinian Arabs

There are many Palestinian Arab professionals working in Israel, and many Israeli Arabs are to be found working as doctors in the main Israeli hospitals and in some areas of the Israeli civil service. Yet real equality is still hard to find.

Human Rights Watch has said Israel operates a 'two-tier' judicial system in those areas of the occupied Palestinian territories it administers, and there are better services and benefits available to Israelis living in settlements in the occupied territories than there are for Arabs, who are under military, not civil, law. Human Rights Watch is right, and it is not antisemitic to say so – it is a legitimate criticism of Israeli policy. The Israeli authorities recognise that they provide differential treatment for Palestinians and Israelis – there are, for instance, separate roads for each community plus checkpoints for Palestinians – but they argue in their defence that the measures are necessary to protect Israelis from attacks by Palestinian armed groups.

Equally, the criticism from within and outside Israel of racism and discrimination against minority groups within Israel is not antisemitic. Much of the criticism has been shrugged off by the Israeli government, but their own Or Commission (in 2000, after civil unrest at the beginning of the second intifada)[28] plus the United States Department of State, have published reports that document racism and discrimination against specific racial and ethnic groups within Israel.

A study commissioned by Israel's Courts administration and the Israel Bar Association demonstrated that Arab Israelis who have been charged with certain types of crime are more likely than their Jewish counterparts to be convicted, and once convicted they are more likely to be sent to prison.[29] This is clearly discriminatory, and calling that out is legitimate.

It is clear too that Israeli anti-discrimination employment laws in Israel are rarely enforced. Saying so is not antisemitic. There is a coalition of nine Israeli rights groups that have come together to oppose the practice of allowing companies to advertise their policy of hiring only Jewish Israelis, not Arab Israelis. And they do that because they oppose the unofficial policy of making Israel more Jewish – and we are right to call that out too.

So the question of whether criticisms of Israel and the actions of its government are always to be considered antisemitic is a complicated, extremely fraught issue. As we have seen, many criticisms are entirely justified, provided they are criticisms of policy. But some have, at the very least, an antisemitic undertone. When they echo centuries old antisemitic lies – the blood libel, the Protocols of the Elders of Zion – it is hard to see how they can be anything else. When they target Israel and no other country, it is reasonable to ask why Israel attracts such hatred. Is antisemitism behind that? The BDS movement trying to render anything Israel-related toxic is a case in point. The shrill slogan-calling of 'apartheid', 'genocide' and 'ethnic cleansing' against the Israeli government is a case in point. Apart from the accusations being untrue, they have a particular echo of horror for Jews, as a result of the Holocaust when it was the Jews who were ethnically cleansed and were the victims of genocide.

Though some in power within Israel do not like to admit it, criticism of Israel comes from Jews and non-Jews alike, including from organisations such as the New Israel Fund, which some on the Israeli right would like to silence. And those who support the New Israel Fund, and support all sorts of other organisations in Israel, its universities, its think tanks, its NGOs, including many people who love Israel and live there, nevertheless feel it is not only fair but often right to criticise some of what is going on. Many of the fiercest critics are themselves Jews. Of course they defend Israel's right to exist, and are proud of 'brave little Israel', as it was described after the audacious 1976 Entebbe rescue by the Israeli paramilitary brigades of over a hundred hostages hijacked by a group of Palestinian and German militia. They are proud of all its achievements. But they become angry when some in the Israeli government or civil society want to suppress criticism of Israel, whether at home or abroad, whether justified or not.

We can see very clearly why attacking all Jews for the policies of the State of Israel is so ridiculous, because Jews themselves do not speak with one voice, either in Israel or beyond. The old Jewish saying: 'Two Jews, three opinions' is no joke – the variety and shades of opinion is a fact.

Israel is an admirable, creative country, with astonishing cultural and culinary inventiveness, a buzzing gay scene, a vibrant intellectual community, a diverse religious life, and with extraordinary scientific and technological creativity. But it has been ruled for many years (with little sign of change) by a government that plays to fears, that is in hock to the religious right, that claims to speak for the whole Jewish people but cannot reasonably do so, and where asylum seekers are less than well treated, let alone West Bank and Gazan Palestinians. The extent to which you feel either of these statements caps the other depends on your standpoint. Like most countries, Israel has good and bad, but what is remarkable is that 'brave little Israel' has stood the test of time. Now its challenge is to make peace with its neighbours, to win back the respect of much of the world, while keeping its friends, trying not to alienate them, and convincing its enemies that it is here to stay and wants to make peace. Will that happen in my lifetime? I doubt it, and yet stranger things have happened.

Attacks in Europe: Who is to Blame?

In March 2012, just outside the Ozar haTorah School in Toulouse, Rabbi Jonathan Sandler and three children, two of them his, were shot dead. At first it was thought that the attacker was a deranged lone neo-Nazi. But nine days later, a journalist at France 24 picked up the phone to a caller who claimed responsibility. He said he was linked to al-Qaeda and that his aim was to protest against the French law banning the veil, and to take revenge on the French army for its presence in Afghanistan and on the Israelis for the killing of Palestinian children. The police found the man responsible, Mohammed Merah, heavily armed, and having been radicalised by al-Qaeda leader al-Zawahiri. Al-Zawahiri hates France. Merah hates Jews. It was a perfect storm.

A few years later, in the summer of 2014, Molotov cocktails were lobbed into the Bergische synagogue in Wuppertal, Germany, a synagogue previously destroyed on Kristallnacht. A Berlin imam, Abu Bilal Ismail, called on Allah to 'destroy the Zionist Jews . . . Count them and kill them, to the very last one.'

At the time, academics and Jewish leaders believed the attack was more than simply a reaction to the conflict in Gaza; the threats, hate speech and violence were an expression of a much deeper and more widespread antisemitism that has been growing now in Germany for more than a decade. Some of that antisemitism comes from Muslims. But some comes from the far right of the political spectrum, as the rise of the AfD (Alternative für Deutschland) makes clear. 'These are the worst times [in Germany] since the Nazi era,' Dieter Graumann, then president of Germany's Central Council of Jews, told the *Guardian*.

On the streets, you hear things like 'the Jews should be gassed', 'the Jews should be burned' – we haven't had that in Germany for decades. Anyone saying those slogans isn't criticising Israeli politics, it's just pure hatred against Jews: nothing else. And it's not just a German phenomenon. It's an outbreak of hatred against Jews so intense that it's very clear indeed.[30]

Indeed, the Minister President of North Rhine-Westphalia, Armin Laschet, has made it clear that while antisemitism is growing both among the far-right and among Muslim migrants in Germany, the larger threat is posed by right-wing extremists.[31] The far-right AfD party has been widely accused of fomenting hate against refugees, Muslims and Jews, and Alexander Gauland, the party's co-leader, has described the Holocaust as a 'small bird dropping in over 1,000 years of successful German history'. Figures make it clear that an overwhelming majority of any violence against Jews in Germany is perpetrated by far-right supporters. 'Militant right-wing extremists are now openly calling for the desecration of Jewish institutions and attacks against Jewish people,' according to Petra Pau, an MP for Germany's Die Linke party, who also said more and more people felt free to 'deny the Holocaust and engage in antisemitic agitation'.[32]

In 2018, the German city of Chemnitz was the epi-centre of fierce clashes as anti-migrant protests and counter-protests escalated. Thousands marched through the streets following the arrest of two men, an Iraqi and a Syrian, over the fatal stabbing of Daniel Hillig, a thirty-five-year-old German-Cuban. The violence was largely directed against Angela Merkel's handling of the 2015 migrant crisis, with far-right activists demonstrating against immigration into Germany. The Foreign Minister Heiko Maas felt it necessary to voice his support for those marching against the far-right supporters: 'The Second World War started 79 years ago. Germany caused unimaginable suffering in Europe. If once again people are parading today in the streets making Nazi salutes, our past history forces us to resolutely defend democracy.'[33] An unhappy situation.

Chemnitz mayor Barbara Ludwig spoke out against the far-right demonstrations and urged Germany to defeat the anti-migrant sentiment: 'We won't allow for the right and right-wing thinking to undermine the state.'[34]

But the AfD, now second in the polls after Angela Merkel's coalition, shared the anti-migrant view of the demonstrators. It also contains serious antisemitic elements. Jan Riebe of the Amadeu Antonio Stiftung, an antiracist, anti-extremist research and campaigns organisation in Germany, conducted extensive research on the party and summarised the situation as follows:

> The AfD is not a genuinely anti-Semitic party. That would mean that the party is actually being held together by anti-Semitic sentiments, but this is not the case. However, many AfD members do share anti-Semitic ideas; they have an anti-Semitic view of the world, meaning that they believe that Jews are the masterminds of all evil ... You can always find clearly anti-Semitic remarks made by AfD members on the internet – for example, on Facebook ... it is also popular within the AfD to blame Jews, in general or as individuals, for migration to Europe – i.e., the refugees who come to Europe. It is said that this is a Jewish plan. Familiar anti-Semitic stereotypes can repeatedly be found within the AfD ...[35]

The examples continue, and are disturbing, given AfD's success electorally, given that it is now a mainstream German political force. Germany's history makes it all the more troubling when it appears, despite all Germans learning about the Holocaust in school, that their knowledge of Germany's recent past has not inhibited stereotypical antisemitic views.

So there is the new rise of antisemitism on the right, and there is also currently a significant issue with Islamic antisemitism, often in the same countries in Europe, notably France and Germany, with considerable hatred preached in some mosques around the world, particularly relating to the State of Israel, though many mosques have close links with synagogues, and many Muslims are among the first to speak out against antisemitism and antisemitic attacks.

Nationalisms

One of the accusations frequently levelled at Jews is that they are not proper Brits, Germans or Americans, or that they have conflicting loyalties. Many Jews (and many others) were disturbed by Prime Minister Theresa May's now infamous line about 'citizens of the world' being 'citizens of nowhere' at the Conservative Party Conference in 2016 for this very reason: 'If you believe you're a citizen of the world, you're a citizen of nowhere. You don't understand what the very word "citizenship" means.'

In response, Henry Mance, a political correspondent for the *Financial Times*, tweeted a picture of a letter in his paper,[36] from Londoner Jem Eskenazi, a 'self-confessed citizen of the world':

Anybody with an ounce of intelligence understands that climate change, pollution or epidemics know no frontiers, that extreme poverty in one region has stability implications for the whole world; that terrorism is a global problem with global solutions; [wars] are not started by citizens of the world but narrow-minded people with a blind belief of their superiority, that some of the greatest minds in any society are descendants of immigrants and refugees ... I do understand very well what citizenship is, Mrs May. It is to have a balanced view of the interests of your family, your neighbourhood, your town, your country and your world.

Eskenazi added that nearly half of Britons agree with the statement that they are more a 'global citizen' than a citizen of their country: 'You have told us we are citizens of nowhere. And this from the pulpit that says "A country that works for everyone".'[37]

What Theresa May perhaps did not understand was that her words echoed a pejorative sense of cosmopolitanism, which has its roots in Russian and German antisemitic discourse of the nineteenth century, where the 'rootless Jew' was seen as a 'cosmopolitan' citizen from 'nowhere', harking back to the old 'wandering Jew' legend. That, like the blood libel, seems first to have occurred as a term, indeed a story, in England, in the works of Roger of Wendover from 1228, under the title 'Of the Jew Joseph who is still alive awaiting the last coming of Christ'. The myth spread. In German and Russian, he is known as *Ewiger Jude*, the 'Eternal Jew'. In French he is *le Juif errant*, 'the wandering Jew'. But the legend – as far as we can see – goes back earlier than Roger of Wendover.

As early as 400 CE Aurelius Prudentius Clemens (b. 348) wrote in his Apotheosis:

> From place to place the homeless Jew wanders in ever-shifting exile, since the time when he was torn from the abode of his fathers and has been suffering the penalty for murder, and having stained his hands with the blood of Christ whom he denied, paying the price of sin.[38]

By the mid-twentieth century, just after the Holocaust, the term 'wandering Jew' was used to refer mostly to Jewish intellectuals, suggesting their lack of patriotism, their non-belonging. The 'modern' campaign against so-called 'rootless cosmopolitans' began in 1946, when Joseph Stalin attacked writers who were ethnic Jews. This was part of the Soviet antisemitic campaign of 1948–53, and became a big issue.

It culminated in the 'exposure' of what turned out to be the non-existent 'Doctors' plot', after a bad five years up to that point. A group of predominantly Jewish doctors from Moscow were accused of conspiring to assassinate Soviet leaders, and various antisemitic articles were being published in the state media at the time. The press articles pointed to threats from Zionism and then proceeded to condemn people with Jewish names. Many doctors, officials and others, Jews and non-Jews alike, were dismissed from their jobs and arrested. A few weeks later, after the death of Stalin, the new Soviet leadership stated there was no evidence to be found, and dropped the case. Soon after, the whole thing was declared to have been fabricated.

But the expression 'rootless cosmopolitan' did in fact come from Russia originally. It was coined in the nineteenth century by the Russian literary critic Vissarion Belinsky, to describe writers who lacked Russian national character.[39] This became serious stuff once again under Stalin. The Russian satirical periodical *Krokodil* published a caricature of the 'rootless cosmopolitan' in March 1949, depicting a travelling writer, with caricatured Jewish features, being described negatively as a 'passportless drifter' for whom writing is a weapon – he wears a pen shaped like a knife on his belt and carries ink in a cartridge marked with a skull and crossbones. This 'cosmopolitan' writer, with his mismatched European and American clothing, is considered a threat to the local community because he produces 'slander against Russian art' and 'slander against Soviet Culture'. The cartoon image is subtitled by a quotation from Belinsky: 'I must admit that I find pathetic and unpleasant those detached skeptics, abstract little men, passportless drifters among humanity.'[40]

No wonder many Jews found Theresa May's words disturbing. So what, or who, is a Jewish rootless cosmopolitan? These identity questions are complicated. First of all, there was no Jewish state after 70 CE until 1948, so Jews were loyal citizens or subjects of wherever they happened to live. Sometimes they were not so loyal because of how they were treated, and sometimes – all too often until the nineteenth century – they were not citizens, because they did not have full civil rights. But once Jews did achieve full civil rights in much of Europe, they became exceptionally loyal citizens.

It did not stop that loyalty being called into question. One of the accusations the Nazis often levelled at German Jews was that they did not volunteer to fight in the First World War. But this turns out to be completely untrue, just like most of what the Nazis said.

An estimated 100,000 German Jewish military personnel served in the German Army during the Great War. The Iron Cross was awarded to 18,000 German Jews during the war – including my own grandfather. And of the 100,000 Jews who served with the German military, 70,000 fought at the front line, 12,000 were killed in action, and 3,000 were promoted to officer ranks – but they could only become officers of the reserve, not the regular army. What is so sad is that Jews in Germany were subject to accusations of disloyalty despite the number of volunteers coming forward.

In 1916, the German General Staff ordered a census, *Judenzählung*, of all Jewish soldiers in the army, to determine how many served on the front line. The fabricated census was publicised with great fanfare, suggesting that the Jews were shirking their duty. However, the actual results showed that 80 per cent of all Jewish soldiers served on the front lines, far higher than among the general population. That result – shamefully – was never released to the general public. And the fact of this census disgusted many German Jewish soldiers, being aimed at proving – falsely – that Jews were trying to avoid military service. But they also had strong patriotic feelings towards Germany – they were citizens of somewhere, not the world. But alas, not for long.

The idea behind this accusation of Jews being rootless cosmopolitans is that Jews, instead of being loyal subjects, proper Brits or Germans or Russians or Frenchmen and women, are actually 'world citizens, seeking to dominate it'. This was the canard published in the faked Protocols of the Elders of Zion.

Take just one example of literally thousands of these accusations of world domination to be found with a quick Google search: the so-called 'Real Jew News', propounded by someone, born Jewish, calling himself Brother Nathanael Kapner. He argues that 'Jews control the world', and his 'news' is much copied. This is just an extract of what he cites as 'the truth':

1649: Jews finance Cromwell's beheading of Charles I. Cromwell reciprocates by allowing Jews to return to England.

1697: London Stock Exchange becomes the world's largest 'purse'. Twelve ruling seats are reserved for Jews only.

1750: The Jew, Mayer Amschel Rothschild, becomes prime money lender to the Crown. The Rothschilds are still in the Frankfurt ghetto.

1848: Jews demand that the Gentiles turn over their property to them through the book *The Communist Manifesto* written by Rothschild-agent, Karl Marx.

1890: The largest munitions factory in the world, Vickers of England, is established by the Rothschilds. The stage is set for the Rothschilds' engineering of World War I and all future wars.

1906: Guglielmo Marconi's invention of the radio is marketed and taken over by the Jew, David Sarnoff. Sarnoff establishes the Marconi Company in England and RCA in America. Thus begins the Jewish control of the media.

1910: Jews take over the office of Minister of Finance throughout Europe. Louis Klotz becomes Minister of

Finance of France; Michael Luzzati of Italy; Bernhard Dernburg of Germany; Rufus Isaacs of England; and Djavid Bey of Turkey. All Jews.[41]

But, just like the other so-called 'facts' Kapner adduces, this last allegation has no basis in fact. The truth is that they were not all Jews. Some were, and some had Jewish ancestry, but they were very different individuals. Klotz was determinedly anti-German, responsible for negotiating reparations from Germany after the First World War. Luigi Luzzati was very briefly minister of finance of Italy a decade or more earlier, not Michael. Bernhard Dernburg was a Protestant. Rufus Isaacs was never a finance minister, and Djavid Bey was of Dönmeh descent, which means that his family may have been crypto Jews, but he certainly was not. These inaccuracies matter because this so-called 'fact' of five Jewish finance ministers in Europe after 1910, with the implication that they were 'in it together' for their own ends, is to be found again and again on the internet and elsewhere, never, ever, corrected.

Kapner's list ends with 'The Stage Is Set for World-Wide Jewish Domination! Only A Christian Revival Can Stop The Jews!' Would that he were simply an isolated, deluded conspiracy theorist. Sadly, he is by no means alone. There are hundreds upon hundreds of such posts, often white supremacist, often claiming Christian hegemony, to be found on the internet – and any number who believe Jews are not proper Brits or Americans, and that there is a real-world Jewish conspiracy.

Yet arguing that Jews are not proper Brits, Germans, Frenchmen, goes back further and it leads not only to accusations of disloyalty but also to the idea that Jews control the media, the banks, politics, all for their own ends. This was, of course, a key part of Nazi ideology. What is so distressing is that these theories about control and world Jewish domination are all too pervasive once more. Truth no longer matters, and conspiracy theories can fester and flower. A survey in December 2018 found that 95 per cent of British Jews consider it antisemitic if someone does not consider Jews living in the UK to be British nationals.[42] But the fact that ideas are swirling about on the internet about Jews lacking loyalty and being 'in it together' against national interests is deeply disturbing, and certainly antisemitic.

Money and Media

At various points in history Jews have been thought to control the markets and to have set up all the banks. Jews were indeed moneylenders in much of Christian Europe in the medieval period. This was because Christian legislation forbade them from farming or owning land, and simply made it impossible to access craftsmen's guilds. Local rulers and church officials closed many professions to the Jews, pushing them into marginal occupations considered socially inferior, such as tax and rent collecting and moneylending, and tolerated them as a 'necessary evil'. Since few other occupations were open to them, Jews took up moneylending.

The charging of interest, known as usury, was banned by Christian churches. This included charging a fee for the use of money, such as at a bureau de change. All this derives from the Hebrew Bible:

Deuteronomy 23:19: Thou shalt not lend upon interest to thy brother: interest of money, interest of victuals, interest of anything that is lent upon interest.

Deuteronomy 23:20: Unto a foreigner thou mayest lend upon interest; but unto thy brother thou shalt not lend upon interest; that the LORD thy God may bless thee in all that thou puttest thy hand unto, in the land whither thou goest in to possess it.

Israelites were forbidden to charge interest on loans made to other Israelites, but they were allowed to charge interest on transactions with non-Israelites, as such transactions could also allow interest to be charged between Israelites via a third party, a non-Israelite, for the purpose of business. Debt was to be avoided and not used to finance consumption, only when absolutely needed.

But it was the interpretation that interest could be charged to non-Israelites that would be used in the fourteenth century for Jews living within Christian societies in Europe to justify lending money for profit. This conveniently sidestepped the rules against usury in both Judaism and Christianity, as the Jews could lend to the Christians, and the Christians were not involved in the lending but were still free to take the loans.

The fact that Jews became moneylenders led to them being described as insolent, greedy usurers. The very unpleasant term to 'Jew' or to 'Jew someone down', meaning to bargain hard and unfairly, derives from this. There were considerable tensions between creditors (typically Jews) and debtors (typically Christians), and when the Black Death epidemics devastated Europe in the mid-fourteenth century, annihilating more than half of the population, Jews were the scapegoats, maybe partly related to the fact that people owed them money. Rumours spread that they caused the disease by deliberately poisoning the wells. Hundreds of Jewish communities were destroyed, and although Pope Clement VI tried to protect them, 900 Jews were burnt in Strasbourg in 1348, before the plague had even affected the city! Clement VI condemned the violence and said those who blamed the plague on the Jews had been 'seduced by that liar, the Devil'.

Church legislation restricting the Jews' activities had been in place from the time of the First Crusade. No surprise then to read, in the Fourth Lateran Council of 1215, that: 'Jews may not charge extortionate interest. Jews and Muslims shall wear a special dress to enable them to be distinguished from Christians so that no Christian shall come to marry them ignorant of who they are.'

History tells us why Jews were moneylenders. Not a lot else was open to them. Yet early banking as we would now recognise it is not Jewish at all. It is in fact Italian and Catholic, and dates back to wealthy cities such as Florence, Venice and Genoa in Renaissance Italy. The most famous Italian bank was the Medici bank, established by Giovanni Medici in 1397.

For, gradually, the church's view on usury had softened; Christian families became bankers too, beyond northern Italy. In the sixteenth century, Marrano Jews fleeing from Iberia introduced the techniques of European capitalism, banking and even the concept of state economy to the Ottoman Empire.

In Britain, two immigrant families, Rothschild and Baring, established merchant banking firms in London in the late eighteenth century, which came to dominate world banking in the next century. Rothschilds were Jews. Barings were Lutheran. Both were German. Then, as banking grew in the nineteenth century, many others became involved, including significant numbers of Jews largely from Germany. Many banks were also founded by Quakers: they include the famous clearing banks of Lloyds and Barclays, as well as the smaller specialist banks Fry and Gurney. Declaring that Jews 'control' the financial world was neither true then nor is it true now. It is antisemitic to argue that they do – and suggests that evidence is subjugated to sheer prejudice. Jews are greedy money manipulators, according to this school of thought. Therefore, they must control the banks – even if the evidence suggests otherwise.

Jews are also regularly accused of dominating the media. In America, several film and media outlets are indeed owned by Jews, but to discount Rupert Murdoch, Ted Turner, Silvio Berlusconi, the Hearst group, the Rothermere family, the BBC, the Barclay brothers, Axel Springer, the Bertelsmann family, the *Guardian* group and others is simply absurd. Alleging that Jews control the media is antisemitic. It is both untrue and offensive, and yet again perpetuates an image of some kind of strange Jewish world conspiracy – with Jews in control, weaving their plots internationally, only helping out each other. For, while there are many individual Jews in the media world of various kinds in some countries, they do not act together and many of them are Jewish only insofar as their parents or grandparents happened to be Jews. They often play no role at all in communal Jewish life, and they certainly, as Alan Dershowitz puts it, 'do not conspire to exercise any sort of "Jewish control" over the areas in which they work'.[43]

The writer James Carroll, a Catholic, points out that, although the *New York Times* and the *Washington Post* were founded by families of Jewish origin, 'neither has ever gone out of its way to promote Jewish causes or values. The *New York Times* was derelict, to put it mildly, in reporting on the Holocaust and generally opposed the establishment of Israel . . . It remains critical of many current Israeli policies.' He also describes how Cardinal Óscar Andrés Rodríguez Maradiaga, who was a runner-up for the papacy, blamed the 'Jewish-controlled media' (notably the *Boston Globe*) for the sex scandal that plagued the Catholic Church.'[44]

What Rodríguez Maradiaga failed to mention was that the Jewish community of Boston was very close to, and admiring of, Cardinal Bernard Law, who presided over the archdiocese during the scandal and had worked hard to build bridges between the Catholic and Jewish communities of Boston. None of the leading media critics, lawyers or politicians who railed against the church was Jewish. Most were Catholic. But that didn't seem to matter to the Cardinal, who, like many other anti-semites, believes that if there is a problem 'the Jews' must be to blame. In the words of Carroll again: 'let's stop all this nonsense about Jewish control over the media and praise those individual Jews who, by dint of hard work and talent, have earned their place, as individuals, in so many areas of American life. I always thought that was the American dream.'

There is one further point worth making here. The accusations are about controlling the media, banking and other non-agricultural, non-land-based activities. Hence the idea of Jews being 'rootless cosmopolitans'. Yet Jews, for historical reasons, were often not agricultural people, though there were Jewish agricultural labourers in Europe and Latin America, as well as Israel. I say this as the granddaughter, on my mother's side, of a small-time German Jewish wine grower. Many Jews tend to have had, and have, urban skills. When the professions were opened to them, in nineteenth-century Europe, they flocked to them and did well. Eastern European Jews also had portable skills – think stringed instruments rather than pianos – as well as having been agricultural labourers plus holding other occupations in the Pale of Settlement. There is, among many Jewish families, a real drive for success. James Carroll is right to argue that going for success, ambition, is the great American dream. Criticising Jews for being successful, or blaming them for pointing out, in the course of their work, when things are wrong in the Catholic Church or elsewhere, is of course antisemitic. If Jews reported on problems in the Catholic Church, shooting the messenger because you don't want it to be true, and accusing the Jews of media control, suggests an unwillingness to face the truth, and a preference for shifting blame on to those who carry centuries of prejudice already. If Jews are to be criticised for being too successful – and, of course, many Jews are not 'successful' in that sense – then the Enlightenment idea that education and personal effort can take you a long way needs to be re-examined. Jews have simply taken advantage of what is available and, like many other minority groups, have overwhelmingly valued education and what it brings.

Denial of the Holocaust

Another example of what is, without doubt, a form of current antisemitism that is widespread on social media and elsewhere is denial that the Holocaust ever happened, or a diminution, and disparaging, of its scale. It happens, presumably, because denying the Holocaust denies the most recent, and most terrible, destruction of Jewish people on a hitherto unimaginably vast scale. It matters because it allows the argument to proceed that Jews 'use' or 'weaponise' the Holocaust to defend 'their' actions in the Middle East, or in the media or banks or wherever. It matters because by denying history, you deny the experience of thousands of people still alive who survived, and you deny a group memory and awareness among Jews of what was done to them (and others) in the name of an unspeakable ideology.

It appears that 1 in 20 people in the UK do not believe the Holocaust ever took place, as polling to coincide with Holocaust Memorial Day 2019 discovered.[45]

Every child in Britain covers the Holocaust in a history class at some stage in the curriculum. Holocaust studies, once a rare subject, is now commonplace within universities, particularly in the United States. Novels focusing on the Second World War are many in number. Serious works of highly acclaimed popular history that deal with the Holocaust in some way or other are widely available.

People know about the Holocaust, and about what led up to it. They know about the few heroes, and they know about the Nazi machine. They see news stories about the last of the Nazi war criminals being tried in court, and they read endless fiction portraying the Nazis as utterly evil. Many young people visit Auschwitz in their sixth form year, and they visit the Holocaust exhibits at the Imperial War Museum or the Holocaust Centre in Nottingham.

And yet – despite the prevalence of information, museums, records and factual evidence – Holocaust denial not only exists, it may in fact be growing. Scan the Twittersphere and it's widespread. Daniel Finkelstein wrote in the *Jewish Chronicle* in April 2016:

> Let me give you some examples of tweets sent to me (with my name tagged) in the last two days. 'The holocaust is a lie #Hitlerwasright'; 'The holocaust is a complete fake'; 'What holocaust', 'Hollow cost'; 'Count up the deaths throughout the middle east and then talk to me about holocaust maties'; 'Finkelstein, what a wonderful traditional English name' ... As I say, that's just the last two days. Some of the people tweeting this sort of stuff have a handful of followers, but many have hundreds and some have thousands. One particularly obnoxious individual, Charles Frith, who spreads Holocaust (or as he calls it 'holohoax') denial has tens of thousands of readers. His particular speciality is linking child abuse, mad anti-Zionist nonsense and holocaust denial in a constant stream.[46]

Or there is the explanation of why Holocaust denial matters in these Twitter responses countering Mark Zuckerberg's reluctance to remove such posts from Facebook:

> Holocaust denial is not a 'mistake', Mr. Zuckerberg. It has a clear purpose: negate, distort, minimize, and

trivialize proven facts about the Nazi genocides against Jews, Roma, and others. The goal is to rehabilitate the racist, anti-Semitic, xenophobic ideology of Nazism . . . In order to remove the political taint from Nazism they argue: (1) The Holocaust didn't happen (2) The Holocaust happened but not that many Jews were murdered (3) The Holocaust happened but Hitler didn't do it (4) The evidence was made up by Jews. These CAN'T go together.[47]

And yet, some people do believe all this together. They suspend their critical faculties. The fact that I can produce scores of photographs of my mother's relatives who were murdered in extermination camps in the early 1940s, because they were German Jews who couldn't flee, is of no interest to these people. Evidence is no longer a trump card. And that is what is so frightening. Opinion ranks as high as evidence, even if the opinion is wrong, craven, vicious or simply absurd.

Those who should rely on evidence, such as the infamous David Irving, previously a so-called historian but now commonly referred to as an author, sometimes decide not to do so, for their own reasons. Mercifully, Irving was defeated in a lawsuit he had brought against the distinguished American historian Deborah Lipstadt, a story beautifully recounted in the 2016 film *Denial*. Irving was totally discredited when, in the course of the case, he was shown to have deliberately misrepresented historical evidence. He was found to be an active Holocaust denier, antisemite and racist, who 'for his own ideological reasons persistently and deliberately misrepresented and manipulated historical evidence'.

Richard J. Evans, former Regius Professor of History

at the University of Cambridge, now Provost of Gresham College in London, was expert witness for the defence, and said this of Irving:

> Irving is essentially an ideologue who uses history for his own political purposes; he is not primarily concerned with discovering and interpreting what happened in the past, he is concerned merely to give a selective and tendentious account of it to further his own ideological ends in the present. The true historian's primary concern, however, is with the past. That is why, in the end, Irving is not a historian.[48]

Irving had always been sympathetic to Hitler and critical of British policy in the Second World War, but his violent Holocaust denial came later. By 1991, in his revised edition of *Hitler's War*, he had removed all references to death camps and the Holocaust. That same year, in a speech given in Hamburg, he said that in two years' time 'this myth of mass murders of Jews in the death factories of Auschwitz, Majdanek and Treblinka ... which in fact never took place' will be disproved. Two days later, he repeated this and praised Rudolf Hess as 'that great German martyr'. Also in 1991, in Canada, he described the Holocaust as a 'hoax', and again predicted that by 1993 the 'hoax' would have been 'exposed'. He expressed his contempt and hatred for Holocaust survivors by proclaiming that:

> Ridicule alone isn't enough, you've got to be tasteless about it. You've got to say things like 'More women died on the back seat of Edward Kennedy's car at Chappaquiddick than in the gas chambers at Auschwitz.'

And he composed an appalling ditty for his young daughter, which he apparently sang to Christopher Hitchens' wife and daughter in their apartment, to their stunned horror:

> I am a Baby Aryan
> Not Jewish or Sectarian
> I have no plans to marry an
> Ape or Rastafarian.[49]

This is revolting stuff, and much of it was quoted during the trial. But while Irving may now be completely discredited, there are very many others out there who share his beliefs.

Take some of the conspiracy theorists, of whom David Icke is perhaps the best known. Icke's politics today are a combination of most of the dominant themes of contemporary neo-fascism, mixed in with a smattering of topics culled from the US militia movement, European and Middle Eastern conspiracy theories and most recently (and predictably) Russian state propaganda. In America, for instance, he opposes gun control as a plot by the 'elite', which has deliberately orchestrated numerous mass shootings to whip up opposition to guns. According to the comedian and blogger Marlon Solomon:

> Icke is on a mission to educate and free the subjugated masses; he offers hope and freedom from the grip of our Satanic blood-drinking rulers. He assures us that if we 'can tune into the "Truth Vibrations"' we can rise up as one against the reptilian overlords. The problem is that these overlords are Jewish. Well of course they are . . . Icke is in fact selling out stadiums worldwide . . .

preaching ancient and modern antisemitic conspiracy theories and inciting his bewitched followers to rise up against these – mostly Hebrew – totalitarian overlords ... This is why David Icke is a pin-up for some on the far-right, but, these days, with his antisemitic anti-globalism, he probably has as many acolytes on the fringes of the far-left. Either way, he is undoubtedly a dangerous individual.[50]

Icke has been promoting Holocaust denial since the late 1990s and lost a publishing deal as a result. His website is teeming with links to far-right websites, including to the Institute of Historical Review, a beacon of the international Holocaust denial movement with numerous links to neo-Nazi organisations, and an organisation with which Irving became involved. He has supported notorious Holocaust denier Ernst Zündel under the guise of supporting free speech. The Critical Thinking website wryly observes:

One would imagine however that a more worthy symbol [of free speech] could be found than a pro-Nazi propagandist who has appeared at a trial in a concentration camp uniform and who has disseminated stickers such as 'Holocaust teaching is Child Abuse'.[51]

There is some truly sickening material to be found on Icke's website. And the only country which refused to host Icke for his world tour in 2016 was Germany, where both of his shows, in Stuttgart and Berlin, were cancelled. The fact that Icke's antisemitism and Holocaust denial is not taken seriously is in part a reflection on many people's assessment of him as a likeable fool and a good performer.

But he is allied with the Truthers, with some very unpleasant causes, and his views should be taken seriously by those who book him for events. He is, without doubt, an antisemite.

When Icke's shows in Germany were cancelled, Jan Rathje of the Amadeu Antonio Stiftung, an NGO that tracks racism in Germany, countered the likeable fool caricature: 'David Icke denies the Holocaust, and I think that's more important than focusing on the fact that he sees reptilians in power behind everything.' Icke also supports Alison Chabloz, a neo-Nazi who writes songs mocking Holocaust survivors, who was prosecuted in June 2018 for hate speech, and claimed the Holocaust was 'a bunch of lies'. The fact that this kind of material is in the public domain is sickening. But the more there is, the more some people seem to believe it. Factual evidence is no longer stronger than opinion, in all too many settings.

Icke, Irving, Zündel and many others, including some German historians of the 1960s and 1970s, share these views. This is what led to Richard J. Evans's attack on some of them during the so-called *Historikerstreit*, historical dispute, in Germany. In his 1989 book *In Hitler's Shadow*, he took issue with Ernst Nolte's argument that the Einsatzgruppen massacres of Ukrainian Jews were a justifiable 'preventive security' response to Soviet partisan attacks, as well as attacking his complaints that much scholarship on the Shoah expressed the views of 'biased' Jewish historians. Evans argued that Nolte's views crossed the line into Holocaust denial, and he singled out for particular scorn Nolte's rationalisation that, since the victors write history, the only reason why Nazi Germany is seen as evil is because it lost the war.[52]

Holocaust denial is by no means limited to radicals such as Icke and Irving – and that is what is so terribly disturbing. Back in the 1980s and 1990s, the Université Jean Moulin Lyon 3 was rocked by a series of scandals. It turned out to be the headquarters of the so-called *négationnistes*, Holocaust deniers, a group that was started in the 1970s by Robert Faurisson, an open Holocaust denier, and where the academic staff at the time contained several far-right figures.

In 2002, France's Education Minister Jack Lang commissioned a report on the university by Henry Rousso, the veteran historian of the Vichy government. The report was published in 2004 and turned out to be political dynamite. It showed that professor of Japanese Bruno Gollnisch, who had been Marine Le Pen's number two in the National Front since 2005 and a leading figure in the European Parliament, was at the centre of the *négationniste* group within the university. In 2004, Gollnisch declared that: 'I do not question the existence of concentration camps but historians could discuss the number of deaths. As to the existence of gas chambers, it is up to historians to speak their minds.'[53]

Rousso's 2004 report denounced the complacent attitude of the university with respect to the far-right, which is when Gollnisch reiterated his declarations with their implication of Holocaust denial. The chancellor of the university requested that the Minister of National Education suspend him, and announced the opening of a disciplinary procedure. Gollnisch was suspended for thirty days and excluded from the university, in case of a possible breach of the peace. But that decision was overturned by the Conseil d'État early in 2005, whereupon he started teaching again. There followed a student riot, with students prevented from entering his lectures by groups of other students, both left-wing and Jewish. A group of National Front students blocked the protesters, leading to a brawl and the police arriving. A National Front student was arrested.

At the opening of his trial on 7 November 2006, Gollnisch was asked whether 'the organised extermination of European Jews by the Nazi regime . . . constitutes an undeniable crime against humanity, and that it was carried out notably by using gas chambers in extermination camps'. He replied 'absolutely'. He was finally found not guilty by the Cour de cassation in 2009.

Gollnisch had described the original report by Rousso as politically motivated and a fraud, but was nevertheless fined €55,000 and imprisoned for three months. After that, he was welcomed back by some, which shows how deeply embedded right-wing antisemitism has become in Lyon. The riot had failed. And the mayor of Lyon, Raymond Barre, described him as 'a good servant of Lyon'.[54]

There is no doubt that Holocaust denial is growing, despite attempts to curb it with national events such as Holocaust Memorial Day, when people remember, with lessons in schools and colleges, with material in literature, art, film and elsewhere, with news coverage and harrowing biographical media stories. It is as if, by denying the Holocaust, one can deny Jewish suffering. If Jewish suffering can be denied, then why should the population listen to Jews, or take accusations of antisemitism seriously? If you can argue that it is not true that centuries of antisemitism eventually led to the murder of six million Jews, then you need not address the issue. But the fact is, the evidence is, that it *is* true, and people are alive today who still remember it.

Antisemitism in the Conservative Party

In recent years, there has been more concern in the UK with antisemitism on the left than on the right, even though in fact there is still considerable antisemitism on the far-right, where Jews have always expected it to be. I shall come on to the Labour party shortly, but it is worth remembering, alongside recognising Prime Minister Theresa May's considerable support for the Jewish community, that it was not always like this.

In 2013, Conservative MP Patrick Mercer was caught on camera expressing antisemitic and sexist comments about a female soldier in the Israeli Defence Forces: 'You don't look like a soldier to me. You look like a bloody Jew.' He eventually had to resign because of breaking Parliamentary rules on paid lobbying, but he had a history of racist remarks, of which this was one of the most outrageous.

In 2014, Conservative MP Aidan Burley had to step down as an MP after organising a Nazi-themed stag party in 2012.[55] He had already been sacked as a ministerial aide after he bought a Nazi uniform for the groom to wear during a trip to a French ski resort. He apologised, but the Conservatives said his actions had been 'unacceptable' and he had caused 'deep offence'. The report on the stag party said there had been a Nazi-themed toast during the event, and apparently some of those present also chanted the names of prominent Nazi figures. He was criticised for not making his objections to all this explicitly clear, and while arguing he was neither a racist nor an antisemite, his actions had been 'stupid', and it had been right to remove him from his junior government position. I find it hard to argue that buying a Nazi uniform for someone to wear does not carry a tinge of antisemitism.

Margaret Thatcher was, if anything, a philosemite. She liked her Jewish constituents in Finchley, and she liked having Jews in her Cabinet. She had no patience for antisemitism or for those who countenanced it. 'I simply did not understand antisemitism myself,' she confessed in her memoirs, and she found 'some of [her] closest political friends and associates among Jews.'[56] Nigel Lawson praised her for her lack of antisemitism – and he had the experience to make that judgement. Alan Clark, a senior Tory politician, had written in his diaries that some of the old guard, himself included, thought Lawson could not, 'as a Jew', be offered the position of foreign secretary.[57] And when Thatcher became prime minister, she appointed a government of outsiders. 'The thing about Margaret's Cabinet,' Harold Macmillan would later say, 'is that it includes more Old Estonians than it does Old Etonians.'[58] British Conservative politics, up to that point, had always been a club for genteel gentiles; Thatcher wanted to make it a meritocracy. But that 'Old Estonian' comment was undoubtedly antisemitic. For Thatcher had appointed Keith Joseph, Leon Brittan, Nigel Lawson, David Young and Malcolm Rifkind to her Cabinet, and had other Jews as ministers and advisers as well. The grocer's daughter from Grantham – an outsider herself – did not share either the snobbery or the 'polite' antisemitism of the Tory grandees.

There are other examples of Conservative antisemitism,

particularly in the Macmillan years and shortly after. But more recently, in September 2018, British Conservative MEPs voted against measures to censure Hungary. This was after the European parliament had voted to trigger the EU's most serious disciplinary procedures in response to Hungary's government policies – led by Hungarian Prime Minister Viktor Orbán – to reduce judicial independence and boost control over the media. There were also concerns about corruption in the Hungarian government, and frequent Islamophobic, racist and antisemitic comments.[59]

The September measure was the first use of a so-called Article 7 procedure against a member state, which could, if pursued, see Hungary stripped of its voting rights in the EU. It was narrowly passed by the necessary two-thirds majority – had the Conservative MEPs supported it, it would have gone through more easily. Surprisingly, they were almost alone in their opposition among centre-right parties. Although one cannot argue that they were personally antisemitic or Islamophobic in refusing to support the Article 7 procedure, their action should be questioned, and their unwillingness to speak out against Viktor Orbán and his policies, unlike the other members of their European group, begs a considerable question over where their sympathies lie. Clearly, they should have joined the others in their European group and sent a stronger message that Orbán's policies would not be tolerated.

Jewish and Muslim leaders in the UK spoke out against the MEPs' action, saying it was deeply worrying that they had declined to condemn the repressive policies of the Hungarian Prime Minister. Marie van der Zyl, president of the Board of Deputies, said it was 'very concerning that Conservative party MEPs chose to defend Hungary's appalling track record rather than supporting a motion to uphold the rule of law.' She continued:

> As we have stated previously, we are very alarmed by the messages at the heart of Orbán's election campaign, including his comments about 'Muslim invaders', calling migrants 'poison', and the vivid antisemitism in the relentless campaign against Jewish philanthropist George Soros. This whipping up of prejudice by the Hungarian government, alongside restrictions on press freedom and the independence of the judiciary, must be stopped before it undermines Hungary's democracy irreversibly.[60]

The Muslim Council of Britain's secretary general, Harun Khan, agreed, stating:

> At a time when there are growing concerns about the rise of the far-right across Europe, it is deeply disappointing that Conservative party MEPs were whipped to align themselves with far-right parties in supporting Mr Orbán . . . The Conservative party has thus far resisted calls to have an inquiry into Islamophobia amongst its ranks. This latest action raises further concerns of bigotry in the party.[61]

It was a wonderful example of Jews and Muslims in the UK making common cause. And it was right that they should. For there has been Islamophobia in the Conservative party as well, pointed out firmly by Baroness Warsi, a former chairman of the party.[62] The row has been brewing for some time, and as the Labour party faces constant accusations of antisemitism, so the Conservatives are facing strong accusations of Islamophobia, and have tended to deny them. There is shocking evidence that Islamophobic incidents, comprised of 'language, symbols or actions', had risen 593 per cent in the week after the appalling March 2019 massacre of Muslims at prayer in Christchurch, New Zealand. There is a real problem.[63] When asked about the MEPs' refusal to condemn Orbán's policies, Prime Minister Theresa May's office argued that MEPs make their own decisions, thus distancing itself from the move – hardly adequate as a response, as both Islamophobia and antisemitism are on the rise. One would have expected more from her on this. It seems that neither the Prime Minister nor her MEPs were able to understand why their alliance with Orbán's grouping in the EU should be seen as racist, Islamophobic and antisemitic. And it was particularly surprising that it came from Theresa May, who has on the whole been very supportive of the Jewish community. Yet her creation of a 'hostile environment' for migrants, particularly undocumented migrants, in her time as Home Secretary, has in itself both reflected and probably led to increased xenophobia and mistrust within communities.

The situation with Hungary is complicated – Orbán embraces Bibi Netanyahu, Prime Minister of Israel, while he continues to be violently anti-Muslim. He runs a disgraceful and antisemitic campaign against the billionaire investor George Soros, who was born in Hungary, and refuses to allow in any of the migrants clamouring to reach Europe. The anti-migrant feeling is toxic in Hungary, and Orbán proposes even more restrictive legislation against anyone trying to help them.

Orbán's positioning on migrants may arise from his

reluctance to be outflanked by the popular Hungarian party Jobbik, which received 17 per cent of the vote in the April 2010 national election with their strong anti-migrant pledges. The far-right subculture, which ranges from nationalist shops to radical-nationalist and neo-Nazi festivals and events, has played a major role in the institutionalisation of Hungarian antisemitism in the twenty-first century. Contemporary antisemitic rhetoric may have been updated, but it is still based on familiar antisemitic tropes. The traditional accusations of an international Jewish conspiracy are still wheeled out regularly.

Antisemitism in the Labour Party

During the summer of 2018, the British Labour party tied itself in knots over accusations of antisemitism, which had been simmering since 2015. Ken Livingstone, former Mayor of London, was one high-profile person criticised for antisemitism after drawing crude links between Hitler and Zionism, saying that Hitler had supported Zionism 'before he went mad and ended up killing six million Jews'.[64] Two years after her 2016 report on antisemitism in the Labour party, which many people believe did not go far enough, Shami Chakrabarti, by now Shadow Attorney General, slammed Livingstone for likening Jews escaping Nazis to the Nazis themselves.[65] This was nothing new. Back in 2006 a High Court judge had already argued that Livingstone made 'unnecessarily offensive' and 'indefensible' remarks when he likened a Jewish reporter to a Nazi concentration camp guard. In February 2018, he sparked fury by appearing on Iranian TV on Holocaust Memorial Day to ask whether the genocide has been 'exploited' – as if it were not bad enough already. He also claimed there was a 'well-orchestrated campaign by the Israel lobby to smear anybody who criticises Israel policy as antisemitic'.

Jeremy Corbyn, the party leader, responded to all this by saying: 'We are not tolerating antisemitism in any form whatsoever in our party.' But it took longer than it should have for him to take action against Livingstone. Suspended from 2016, after the investigation, Livingstone was still not expelled from the Labour party for his comments that Hitler was a Zionist. Indeed, in the end Livingstone resigned from the party in 2018 – but without accepting he was guilty of antisemitism. He simply issued a statement claiming he was quitting because his case had become a 'distraction' for Labour under the leadership of Jeremy Corbyn. And it had all gone on so long he did not want to be pushed.

Added to all this, John Mann, a Labour MP who campaigns against antisemitism, was called in by the party leadership because, after those original remarks by Livingstone at the BBC, he had called Livingstone a 'disgusting Nazi apologist'.[66]

What with Livingstone, the Mear One mural and other cases which we will explore below, Corbyn's Labour party was in trouble over antisemitism. They had to do something. Many of their critics – within the Labour party – were urging them to accept the IHRA definition of antisemitism and make it clear they were, finally, serious about it. Yet they dragged their feet – shamefully. The most generous explanation of the reluctance to deal with this ferment of rage and concern about antisemitism on the part of Corbyn and some of his allies may be because they felt that accepting the IHRA definition of antisemitism as it stands could limit what they saw as forthright debate about a resolution to the Israel–Palestine conflict – an issue dear to Corbyn's heart. But much more likely, it is because they wanted to protect the right of people (Palestinians in particular) to be able to describe the Israeli state as 'a racist endeavour' without being branded antisemites, as became clear in discussions held between Jewish communal leaders and Corbyn and his advisers in March 2018.[67]

Meanwhile, the view has been growing among many on the left of the Labour party that the row about anti-semitism is being 'weaponised' and used to undermine Corbyn's leadership. This has been a consistent pattern. Back in 2016, Jonathan Freedland wrote about it very effectively, making it clear that it is not up to the antiracists on the left to decide what antisemitism is:

> On the left, black people are usually allowed to define what's racism; women can define sexism; Muslims are trusted to define Islamophobia. But when Jews call out something as antisemitic, leftist non-Jews feel curiously entitled to tell Jews they're wrong, that they are exaggerating or lying or using it as a decoy tactic – and to then treat them to a long lecture on what anti-Jewish racism really is ... The left would call it misogynist 'mansplaining' if a man talked that way to a woman. They'd be mortified if they were caught doing that to LGBT people or Muslims. But to Jews, they feel no such restraint ... So this is my plea to the left. Treat us the same way you'd treat any other minority. No better and no worse. If opposition to racism means anything, it surely means that.[68]

That 2016 inquiry chaired by Shami Chakrabarti, now Baroness Chakrabarti, found that the party was not 'overrun by antisemitism' but that there was an 'occasionally toxic atmosphere'. Many in the Jewish community found the report inadequate, since, among other things, it did not tackle the growing intimidation of Jewish students within Labour itself, a particular issue in the Oxford University Labour Club where its chairman, Alex Chalmers, resigned publicly in 2016. He cited members of the OULC Executive 'throwing around the term "Zio"', – a derogatory term for Jews usually confined to far-right websites – with 'casual abandon', and 'expressing their "solidarity" with Hamas and explicitly defending their tactics of indiscriminately murdering civilians'.[69]

Baroness Royall, who had been vice-chair of the Chakrabarti inquiry, was asked specifically to look at what was going on in the Oxford University Labour Club. Originally, her report was intended to form part of the Chakrabarti report. When the National Executive Committee decided not to include it, she published it herself, and was scathing about what she found, although she did not believe the Labour Club was institutionally antisemitic.[70]

Nor did the Chakrabarti report tackle in depth the way that some Labour supporters were talking about, and using social media to discuss, Jews. Take the Bognor Regis Labour councillor who posted 'Jews drink blood and rape children' on social media.[71] Or the case of Mohammed Yasin, Labour's West Midlands regional organiser, who was finally suspended in December 2018 after more than two years of offensive social media posts, including 9/11 conspiracy theories, praising a homophobic preacher and blaming 'all wars in the world' on Jewish people – most of which he posted while working in an official capacity for the Labour party.[72]

The launch of the Chakrabarti report in 2016 was packed with Corbyn supporters who were so aggressive that they reduced one very tough Jewish MP, trade unionist Ruth Smeeth, to tears. She later called on Jeremy Corbyn to resign after Marc Wadsworth, an activist with Momentum Black Connexions, publicly accused her of working 'hand-in-hand' with a journalist from what he saw as the right-wing press, the *Daily Telegraph*, presumably pigeon-holing her as an anti-Corbyn right-winger intent on aiding Corbyn's fall from grace. She claimed that the accusation was using 'traditional antisemitic slurs to attack me for being part of a "media conspiracy"' and criticised a lack of response from Corbyn or his office. In his reply to this, Wadsworth said he was unaware that Smeeth is Jewish, as if that were necessarily relevant, with the implication that it would have been fine to say these things if she had *not* been Jewish, and he then refused to apologise. Jon Lansman, one of the founders of Momentum, the group strongly allied to Jeremy Corbyn, commented later in the year: 'It was awful; I was shocked by it. The attack was unacceptable, disgraceful.'[73]

Ruth Smeeth was put under police protection after receiving an antisemitic and homophobic death threat on Facebook. Smeeth said in a BBC Radio interview on 2 September 2016 that she had received 25,000 pieces of abuse since the end of June, including 20,000 in a twelve-hour period. 'It's vile, it's disgusting, and it's done in the name of the leader of the Labour party, which makes it even worse.' According to Smeeth, Corbyn 'should be naming and shaming some of the worst perpetrators who are doing it in his name'. She also stated in the London *Evening Standard* in September 2016 that antisemitic incidents were rare while Ed Miliband was Labour's leader. 'I've never seen anti-Semitism in Labour on this scale,' she said. 'There were one or two incidents before and the reason why they were so shocking is that there were only one or two. Now the sheer volume of it has made it normal.'[74]

Much later, in April 2018, Smeeth was accompanied by a cordon around her of forty or so Labour MPs and peers as she went to a hearing of Labour's National Constitutional Committee into Wadsworth's future in the party. Wadsworth was expelled from membership for bringing the Labour party into disrepute.

And then a couple of important events took place. First, on 25 July 2018, the three main Jewish newspapers, the *Jewish Chronicle*, the *Jewish News* and the *Jewish Telegraph*, united in publishing identical front-page editorials warning of the 'existential' threat to British Jewry that a government led by Jeremy Corbyn would pose:

> We do so because the party that was, until recently, the natural home for our community has seen its values and integrity eroded by Corbynite contempt for Jews and Israel ... The stain and shame of anti-Semitism has coursed through Her Majesty's Opposition since Jeremy Corbyn became leader in 2015.

The editorials outlined the series of scandals and controversies that have beset Labour relating to antisemitism, but they culminated in the debate about accepting the IHRA definition. Labour preferred one that omitted the Israel-related definitions that have become standard elsewhere, and Labour's National Executive Committee had produced its own version of a code on antisemitism.

There are indeed elements of the NEC's version that are arguably preferable. For instance, as Brian Klug has pointed out, it added that 'it is racist to require more vociferous condemnation of Israel's actions from Jewish people or organisations than from others.'[75] Klug added that 'this speaks to the lived experience of some Jewish people on the left.' It also highlighted the antisemitism that consists in making a gratuitous reference to being Jewish (as in 'Jewish banker', comparable to 'black mugger') and Klug adds that neither is present in the IHRA text. That is true. And both these additions might indeed be improvements. But after trying to get rid of the bulk of the definition by the IHRA, the Labour party was in a mess. Its desire to remove the mentions of criticism of Israel, which, where excessive, morph into antisemitism, made it seem unfit for purpose to many within the British Jewish community. In any case, by then, after rows over antisemitism stretching back three years, and a failure to deal with individuals who had expressed antisemitic sentiments in tweets or on Facebook posts, the general consensus, even among Corbyn's immediate team, was that it was too late for Labour to go for its own definition. It was duty bound to accept the IHRA definition.

In September 2018 they finally did accept the definition. But they added an accompanying statement agreed by the NEC aimed at protecting free speech about Israel and the rights of Palestinians. Meanwhile Jeremy Corbyn argued for a more extensive qualifying statement to the definition, saying that 'it should not be considered anti-Semitic to describe Israel, its policies or the circumstances around its foundation as racist because of their discriminatory impact, or to support another settlement of the Israel–Palestine conflict.' But that qualifying statement was rejected out of hand.

The IHRA definition may not be perfection by any means, but what Labour could not and cannot now do, was create their own version that is super-critical of Israel, and allows the vitriolic name-calling that elides into antisemitism, and expect to get away with it. The history of their failure to deal with antisemitism within their own ranks meant that trying to change what had become generally accepted would only open them up to yet more suspicion of apologetic tactics and lack of sincerity.

I will examine the sad history of the Labour party and antisemitism within its ranks here.

Social Media Attacks

The actress Maureen Lipman, known for her role on the long-running soap *Coronation Street*, came under attack from the left in September 2018 after she called Jeremy Corbyn an antisemite. According to the *Daily Mail*, it was 'a plot to stretch credulity even by soap opera standards. Left-wing activists are demanding the removal of Maureen Lipman from *Coronation Street* after she criticised Jeremy Corbyn.'[76]

She has been the victim of a hostile Twitter campaign since her return to the show, and has been variously accused of calling Corbyn supporters 'Holocaust supporters', being 'utterly detestable' and 'vile', displaying 'propaganda in action' and it was said that she needed to be boycotted.

The anonymity and ease of tweeting and posting on Facebook seems to lead to all sorts of racist, misogynistic comments and the vicious trolling of a variety of people. Maureen Lipman is by no means alone in suffering appalling antisemitic abuse. Take the #hodgecomparisons hashtag on Twitter, targeting senior Labour MP for Barking, Dame Margaret Hodge, a secular Jew. In July 2018, the Labour party launched disciplinary action against Hodge, which was later dropped, after an angry public confrontation in which she branded Jeremy Corbyn an antisemite. 'He is now perceived by many as an antisemite,' she told the *Guardian*. 'I chose to confront Jeremy directly and personally to express my anger and outrage. I stand by my action as well as my words. My grandmother and my uncle were murdered by Hitler and many cousins were slaughtered in the gas chambers . . . I joined the Labour party to fight racism. To find myself 50 years later, in 2018, confronting antisemitism in my own party is completely and utterly awful.'[77]

Hodge had compared the investigation into her conduct to the persecution faced by Jews in Nazi Germany, saying she felt 'as if they were coming for me'. Her confrontation with Corbyn left her 'thinking what did it feel like to be a Jew in Germany in the Thirties' and with a 'feeling of fear'.[78]

What followed was a vicious social media whirlwind in which people – including some Labour party members – took pleasure in coming up with 'humorous' alternative versions of Hodge's comparison, which they perceived to be overblown. It was Twitter at its juvenile worst, and it was undermining of the real pain that Hodge felt at the hands of her party, regardless of whether some thought her comparison to 1930s Germany was overplaying the situation.

Some MPs and other senior Labour people, along with many others, have stood up for Margaret Hodge. One Twitter regular, Nick Reeves, commented: 'this is not democratic politics. This is the hate politics that belongs to totalitarianism, not to democracy.'

Margaret Hodge and Maureen Lipman are but two examples of Jews who have come under fire on social media, and have had to endure antisemitic abuse, attacking them as Zionist stooges or mocking and belittling, in Hodge's case, her family's history of either flight from or extermination at the hands of Nazi Germany.

But they are not alone. In September 2018, Metropolitan Police commissioner Cressida Dick was handed a leaked Labour party dossier detailing alleged antisemitism. As a result, Scotland Yard opened a criminal investigation into allegations of antisemitic hate crimes linked to Labour party members. She told the BBC she believed there could be a case to answer and, as a result, the force was consulting with prosecutors on the next steps. The leaked dossier detailed forty-five cases involving messages posted by party members on social media, including one that read: 'We shall rid the Jews who are a cancer on us all.' There was also an entry referring to 'a Zionist extremist MP . . . who hates civilised people, about to get a good kicking'.[79] In March 2019, there were three arrests of former Labour party members on suspicion of publishing or distributing material likely to stir up racial hatred.[80]

A separate and particularly disturbing example came from Mohammed Pappu – once a Labour party rising star – with a series of Facebook posts in which he accused Britain of attacking Syria 'to install a Rothschild bank' and suggested Israel had staged 9/11, the London bombings and the Paris terrorist attacks.[81]

The question that clearly arises through all of this is where are the hate controls on social media? It is a growing cancer, and reading what appears on social media, where all civilised self-limiting restrictions seem to be removed, is both deeply depressing and distressing.

The Mear One Mural

In spring 2018, a row broke out within the Labour party – and subsequently more widely – over the mural by the so-called artist Mear One, which depicts a group of 'hook-nosed' men huddled around a Monopoly-style board, grinding the faces of the poor. The work, Freedom for Humanity, was painted near Brick Lane in London's East End, once a bustling Jewish area, by American graffiti artist Kalen Ockerman, also known as Mear One.

The businessmen and bankers depicted counting their money not only looked like obvious caricatures of Jews – in a style reminiscent of 1930s Nazi propaganda, for it could have come straight out of *Der Stürmer* – but the artist himself confirmed they were intended as such: 'Some of the older white Jewish folk in the local community had an issue with me portraying their beloved #Rothschild or #Warburg etc. as the demons they are.' The mural depicts a classic antisemitic world view of Jews as parasitic capitalists, exploiting the poor, and therefore deserving of no consideration, respect or protection. It harks back to an old antisemitic trope about Jews and money, and anyone with any level of knowledge of history, politics and the world could clearly see that the work was a damning caricature. As Stephen Pollard, editor of the *Jewish Chronicle*, put it: 'Anyone denying that is indulging in sophistry of the most pathetically unconvincing kind.' Indeed, back in 2012, the then Mayor of Tower Hamlets, Lutfur Rahman, ordered council officials to 'do everything possible' to remove the mural, agreeing that 'the images of the bankers perpetuate anti-Semitic propaganda about conspiratorial Jewish domination of financial institutions.'[82]

But when Mr Ockerman wrote on Facebook that his mural was to be removed, a then insignificant backbench Labour MP expressed his support for Ockerman: 'Why? You are in good company. Rockerfeller [sic] destroyed Diego Viera's mural because it includes a picture of Lenin.' Here Jeremy Corbyn was referring to the removal in 1934 of a work by Mexican artist Diego Rivera from the Rockefeller Center in New York.

When the *Jewish Chronicle* unearthed Mr Corbyn's 2012 comment in 2015, it contacted his office for a response, asking about his support for a clearly antisemitic mural remaining on display. No response was forthcoming then or, indeed, for over two years. It wasn't until March 2018, when the Jewish former Labour, now independent, MP Luciana Berger came across the story and asked Mr Corbyn's office for a response, that a spokesman for the Labour leader said: 'In 2012, Jeremy was responding to concerns about the removal of public art on grounds of freedom of speech. However, the mural was offensive, used antisemitic imagery, which has no place in our society, and it is right that it was removed.'

While the statement did acknowledge that the mural was antisemitic, it also claimed that Mr Corbyn was defending it on 'grounds of freedom of speech'. If one follows that argument, it is fine for the leader of the Labour party to support the existence of a large public antisemitic mural, if the result of asking for its removal is judged to be against the principle of free speech. It is hard to believe that Corbyn does not know the difference between freedom of speech and freedom to speak without consequence, so I can only assume that the true explanation for his support of Ockerman is different – he simply could not see anything wrong with the mural.

Corbyn's first response prompted outrage on social media and from a handful of Labour MPs. Ian Austin MP, the adopted child of a Jewish refugee, who had a Labour party investigation against him dropped (over comments he made to the party's chairman about their failure to adopt the internationally recognised definition of antisemitism), tweeted: 'Luciana won't be alone. I think lots of Labour members will want an explanation for this.' Gavin Shuker, MP for Luton South, said that the statement from Corbyn's spokesman 'isn't even an apology. I know this is like screaming into the wind; it'll make zero difference; but I want to state that this is just so wrong. It's impossible to confront anti-Semitism in our party if this is the response from the very top.'

Luciana Berger dismissed the response as 'wholly inadequate'. By this time, even Corbyn's office could see that its 'explanation' had made things worse. A few hours later another statement, this time from Corbyn himself, was issued:

In 2012 I made a general comment about the removal of public art on grounds of freedom of speech. My comment referred to the destruction of the mural 'Man at the Crossroads' by Diego Rivera on the Rockefeller Center. That is in no way comparable with the mural in the original post. I sincerely regret that I did not look more closely at the image I was commenting on, the contents of which are deeply disturbing and antisemitic. I wholeheartedly support its removal. I am opposed to the production of antisemitic material of any kind, and the defence of free speech cannot be used as a justification for the promotion of antisemitism in any form. That is a view I've always held.

If Corbyn is to be believed and he did not look at the mural before responding to the artist's comment on Facebook, he had no business defending it. If in fact he did look at it, his response would indicate that he could see nothing wrong with it – and that is deeply disturbing.

Despite the fact that Corbyn, after much time had lapsed, expressed his 'severe regret' for having questioned why the controversial picture on a wall in East London had to be painted over, many do not believe his explanation. Some feel that it suggests that Corbyn himself might be antisemitic – if he associates Jews with capitalism, he may see himself as a socialist with a duty to oppose capitalist Jews.

Some Labour party members have argued that these accusations of antisemitism are being used by 'elites' to destabilise Jeremy Corbyn's leadership, or that they are being 'weaponised' to allow the right-wing press to attack him. Whether or not that is the case – and I do not believe it is – there is real distress among the Jewish community. A note of antisemitism is being felt within Labour discourse; they can see it in the experiences particularly of Jewish women Labour MPs, they can hear it in Corbyn's own lines about irony or about a cartoon that should have been painted over as soon as it appeared, and they can condemn it because he, and the leadership more generally, do not rush to condemn it. In my view this is not about weaponising, or about elites. This is about a minority that has been rendered insecure by seeing that antisemitic speech and attitudes are tolerated in a major political party, once home to most of Britain's Jewish community, instead of being immediately condemned. It is why Labour-supporting Jews are deserting the party they once loved so dearly. And it is also why, as this book was being put to bed, eight Labour MPs resigned from the party in February 2019, citing both the party's handling of Brexit and institutional antisemitism as their reasons, while more followed, or agonised about remaining.

Conflation of the Terms 'Zionist' and 'Jew'

In the midst of the ongoing row about antisemitism in the British Labour party, a video of Mr Corbyn emerged in summer 2018, in which the Labour leader accuses British Zionists – a term he seemed to use interchangeably with Jews – of having 'no sense of English irony'. The video shows Mr Corbyn in 2013 at a fringe meeting in Parliament for the Palestinian Return Centre, following a speech made by Mr Hassassian, Palestinian Envoy to the UK. In his remarks Corbyn says that 'British Zionists clearly have two problems. One is they don't want to study history, and secondly, having lived in this country for a very long time, probably all their lives, they don't understand English irony either.'[83]

It would, after all, make no sense to say British Zionists, as such, have no sense of irony – Zionism is a political and/or religious belief. When Corbyn says however long 'they' have lived here, he means Jews. And that's what led to the outrage. It is an example of using Zionism as a term to demonise Jews, all the while claiming that he is in no way antisemitic. Yet describing Zionists (read 'Jews') as having no sense of irony – and therefore unlike everyone else – suggests they are not proper Brits, even if they were born here. They are other. Foreign. Unable to share the British sense of humour. That is why the elision of Zionist and Jew is so frightening. It is very dangerous, and horribly seductive for those who do not stop and think.

It is no surprise that many people – Jews and non-Jews alike – were outraged by Corbyn's comment. Lord Sacks told the *New Statesman* that it was 'the most offensive statement made by a senior British politician since Enoch Powell's 1968 "Rivers of Blood" speech . . . it was divisive, hateful and like Powell's speech it undermines the existence of an entire group of British citizens by depicting them as essentially alien.' He continued by saying that Corbyn, by implying 'however long they have lived here, Jews are not fully British,' is using the language of 'classic pre-War European anti-Semitism'.[84] A few days later, Sacks was quoted in the *Independent* as saying that 'Jews have been in Britain since 1656, I know of no other occasion in these 362 years when Jews – the majority of our community – are asking "is this country safe to bring up our children?".'[85]

Many other Jews, me included, think Sacks' comparison with the 'Rivers of Blood' speech was somewhat exaggerated. Sadly, there have been many offensive comments by British politicians since Enoch Powell's speech, including Boris Johnson's comparison of burqa-wearing Muslim women with letterboxes, a strongly Islamophobic remark, and this example of Corbyn's, though appalling, is better countered with acid humour than with outrage.

Take the response from Jonathan Lynn, co-writer of *Yes Minister*, with deadly humour. In his view, the most appropriate response to the Labour leader's denials of antisemitism came from Sir Humphrey Appleby, the programme's fictional Whitehall mandarin: 'Never believe anything until it's been officially denied.' To this, Lynn added: 'I am Jewish. Although I wrote *Yes Minister* and *Yes Prime Minister*, Corbyn says I don't understand English irony. My co-writer Tony Jay was only half-Jewish, so perhaps he half-understood irony and was able to supply some.'[86]

Meanwhile, two Jewish historians and one well-known Jewish novelist and intellectual were at the forefront of the argument about Zionism and the way it is used. In a joint letter published in *The Times* on 6 November 2017, Simon Schama, Simon Sebag Montefiore and Howard Jacobson commented that they were alarmed that, in recent years, 'constructive criticism of Israeli governments has morphed into something closer to antisemitism under the cloak of so-called anti-Zionism.' It is worth quoting their letter at length here:

> We do not object to fair criticism of Israel governments, but this has grown to be indistinguishable from a

demonisation of Zionism itself – the right of the Jewish people to a homeland, and the very existence of a Jewish state ... although anti-Zionists claim innocence of any antisemitic intent, anti-Zionism frequently borrows the libels of classical Jew-hating. Accusations of international Jewish conspiracy and control of the media have resurfaced to support false equations of Zionism with colonialism and imperialism, and the promotion of vicious, fictitious parallels with genocide and Nazism. How, in such instances, is anti-Zionism distinguishable from antisemitism? Zionism – the longing of a dispersed people to return home – has been a constant, cherished part of Jewish life since AD70. In its modern form Zionism was a response to the centuries of persecution, expulsions and mass murder in Christian and Muslim worlds that continued from the Middle Ages to the mid-20th century. Its revival was an assertion of the right to exist in the face of cruelty unique in history. We do not forget nor deny that the Palestinian people have an equally legitimate, ancient history and culture in Palestine nor that they have suffered wrongs that must be healed. We hope that a Palestinian state will exist peacefully alongside Israel. We do not attempt to minimalise their suffering nor the part played by the creation of the state of Israel. Yet justice for one nation does not make justice for the other inherently wicked. Zionism is the right of the Jewish people to self-determination. We believe that anti-Zionism, with its antisemitic characteristics, has no place in a civil society.

The letter was published in the same week that Jeremy Corbyn had refused to attend an event commemorating the centenary of the Balfour Declaration. By contrast, he supplied a video of support for an anti-Balfour march that took place a few days later. Signs carried at that march included a sheet covered with fake bloodstained hands, along with the words 'Zionist media covers up Palestinian holocaust'.

The term 'Holocaust' here is – deliberately and offensively – used in relation to the Palestinians, whose desperate suffering, though terrible, is in no way comparable to the murder of six million Jews and many millions of others at the hands of the Nazis. The media is also accused of being Zionist, for no clear reason. It is clear that the term Zionist here is a code word for Jew.

There is a footnote to all this. In early 2019, the Labour party was beset by yet more issues relating to antisemitism and its leadership's inability – or unwillingness – to deal with it. Among many other instances, in February 2019 the MP Luciana Berger, eight months pregnant, faced two motions of no confidence from her Liverpool Wavertree constituency Labour party. One of her critics had posted on Facebook that the MP should be 'exposed for the disruptive Zionist she is'.

The motions were withdrawn, after strong pressure from the leadership – for which, strangely, they refused to take credit. Deputy leader Tom Watson MP did ask for the constituency party to be suspended, however. Yet the executive of the Liverpool Wavertree constituency Labour party rejected accusations of political bullying, and said claims of antisemitism were a 'false and slanderous accusation'.

Watson said: 'She's being bullied. That motion should never have been moved in her local party, the meeting to hear it should never have been scheduled.' Former Labour Prime Minister Tony Blair also called condemned Berger's treatment: 'The fact that someone like Luciana Berger – who is a smart, capable, active member of parliament doing her best for her constituents – the fact that she should even be subject to a no-confidence motion with this type of allegation swirling around is shameful for the Labour party.'[87]

Alongside this, many Labour MPs had asked the ruling National Executive Committee to declare how many accusations and complaints of antisemitism it had received. They proceeded to attack the party leadership's response after senior officials admitted that only 12 of almost 700 reports of alleged anti-Jewish abuse had resulted in members being expelled. Of the 673 cases of members reported for alleged antisemitism between April 2018 and January 2019, almost a third were dropped without further action, and only 42 were referred to the party's disciplinary arm, the National Constitutional Committee.

Dame Margaret Hodge MP cast doubt on the figures. She herself had submitted 200 of what she considered to be the most serious cases of antisemitism against her, which made the 679 total figure look woefully small: 'It's unbelievable. Trust has broken down. The only people who can put it back are the leadership – it can only come back through the leadership, it can't come back in any other way. [But] Jeremy wasn't there last Monday, he failed to put out any message of support to Luciana [Berger] over the weekend, and he chose not to come tonight. That says it all.'[88]

Just as this book was going to print, the *Sunday Times*

disclosed that the backlog of complaints about antisemitism in the Labour party was so great officials could not
act on them quickly, and that, despite denial, there was
interference from Jeremy Corbyn's office in relation to
those complaints that were addressed.[89] The *Sunday Times*
leader commented: 'It has come to a sorry pass when the
election of a Labour government is a prospect viewed
with genuine fear by many in the Jewish community. They
are afraid that the culture of anti-Semitism in Labour is
growing and that the party's response is to sweep it under
the carpet. That is another outrage.'[90]

In mid-February 2019, when eight senior Labour
MPs broke away from the Labour party, they cited antisemitism within the party as one of the main reasons.
One of them, Luciana Berger, who had been mercilessly
bullied and attacked as a Jew, said Labour had become
institutionally antisemitic and she was 'embarrassed and
ashamed' to stay. Another, Chuka Umunna, had been
pressing the Labour leadership to do something about
antisemitism in the party for a year.

Some MPs have left. More may go. But it is extraordinary that the Labour party should now feel to so many
people as if it is institutionally antisemitic, and apparently
not be prepared to do anything about it. For only a week
after first eight, then nine, Labour MPs resigned from
the Labour party over antisemitism and its handling of
Brexit, Labour MP Chris Williamson said, at a meeting
of Momentum in Sheffield, that Labour had 'given too
much ground' in the face of criticism over antisemitism,
and that it had been 'demonised as a racist, bigoted party'.
He later half-apologised, but meanwhile, after a number of
Labour MPs called for his suspension, he was suspended

'pending investigation'. Deputy leader Tom Watson has acknowledged the problem, while John McDonnell, the shadow chancellor, also admitted the Labour party had a deep problem with antisemitism. He said that the party 'clearly' has issues with anti-Jew hate and that it had to be eradicated, though he suggested only 0.1 per cent of the party membership were involved. One might say 0.1 per cent is too many by far, particularly in an avowedly antiracist party. And to add to that, the Equality and Human Rights Commission had begun pre-enforcement proceedings, precursor to a full statutory investigation, against the Labour Party over antisemitism, just as this book went to press.

My Labour-supporting parents would be turning in their graves.

Violence and Vandalism

Violence driven by antisemitism, and the vandalism of buildings and gravestones, may still be at a low level in the UK but it is increasing, and it is of course very worrying.

The Community Security Trust (CST), a Jewish organisation that provides security for the Jewish community and monitors antisemitism, recorded 1,382 antisemitic incidents in 2017, the highest annual total they had ever recorded, a 3 per cent increase on 2016, and that was exceeded once again in 2018 with a total of 1,600 incidents, a further 16 per cent increase. Previous record high annual totals in 2014 and 2009 occurred when conflicts in Israel and Gaza caused steep, identifiable 'spikes' in antisemitic incidents recorded by CST. In contrast, in 2016, 2017 and 2018 there was no sudden, statistically outlying large spike in incidents that could explain the overall record high. But something has changed.

CST argue that it is likely that there is under-reporting of antisemitic incidents to both their organisation and the police, and that the number of antisemitic incidents that took place is significantly higher than the number they recorded.

Between 2006 and 2016, reported antisemitic incidents surpassed 100 per month on only six occasions. Since April 2016, there have been under 100 incidents reported in only two months in total. This is how racism works. It grows. It is insidious. The pro-Brexit vote was not antisemitic in itself, but it is clear that it emboldened racists, and it is hard not to draw the conclusion that it emboldened antisemites too.

These are not such minor incidents as to be meaningless – they encompass the daubing of swastikas on gravestones, minor attacks on Jewish buildings, the sending of hate mail to prominent Jews, anonymous phone calls and abusive posts on Twitter and Facebook, and so on. Not only is it seriously unpleasant, it can also lead to fear and the need for protection for targeted individuals.

While we are thankfully yet to see serious violence driven by antisemitism here, that sadly isn't the case outside the UK. I want to focus on a few examples, to illustrate why it is so important that when violent crimes are motivated by antisemitism, that it is recognised as such.

In Paris in 2006, Ilan Halimi, a young Frenchman of Moroccan Jewish ancestry was kidnapped by a group calling itself the 'Gang of Barbarians'. The kidnappers, who believed that all Jews are rich, repeatedly contacted the victim's modestly placed family demanding large sums of money. Halimi was held captive and tortured for three weeks before he was thrown by the side of the road and left to die.

The police came under criticism for not understanding the antisemitic nature of the kidnapping. Their decision to keep certain matters secret during the time Halimi was captive was seen as counter-productive and may have prevented a facial composite of one of the key perpetrators being issued. When the police finally released a facial composite picture, a woman turned herself in to the police and pointed to the Barbarians, a gang of African and North African immigrants who had perpetrated similar abductions in the past. After that, French police arrested fifteen people in connection with the crime. The leader of the gang, Youssouf Fofana, who had been born in Paris to parents from Côte d'Ivoire, fled to his parents' homeland.

On 26 February 2006, tens of thousands of people marched through the streets of Paris, demanding justice for Halimi. The kidnapping brought many Jews to speak out against antisemitism and racism, but also stirred discussion about whether Jews could still feel safe in France. Some felt they could not, and there is evidence that immigration to Israel by French Jews in the ensuing months rose as a result. Between 2006 and 2016, some 40,000 French Jews emigrated, though fear may be only one motivating factor, as jobs and financial security also play a part.[91]

The perpetrators of Halimi's abduction were tried and brought to justice in 2009. But, to the anger of many Parisian Jews, the Chirac government dissembled and chose to ignore the antisemitic quality of the murder and torture. Andrew Hussey, in his book *The French Intifada*, commented that 'Only Nicolas Sarkozy, then an ambitious minister of the interior, whose mother was a Sephardi Jew, denounced the murder of Ilan as an "anti-Semitic crime".'[92]

Fast forward a few years later to July 2014 and again in France – this time in the Paris suburb of Sarcelles, a synagogue was firebombed by a 400-strong mob, and a Jewish owned pharmacy was burnt down. The day before, 3,000 people, mostly but not entirely Arab and North African young men, had gathered near the Gare Du Nord train station and begun marching up Boulevard Barbès, leading to police injuries and several arrests. A week earlier, an anti-Israel demonstration in Bastille Square had turned violent, with protesters seeking out and attacking Jewish targets and screaming 'death to the Jews' and 'Hitler was right.'

So heightened was the antisemitic feeling that the French Jewish artist and activist, Ron Agam, asked: 'Over the last few days in France are we seeing the beginning of a French Kristallnacht?'[93] Anti-Israel riots followed for many weeks. A kosher supermarket and pharmacy were smashed and looted; the crowd's chants and banners included 'Death to Jews' and 'Slit Jews' throats'. That same weekend, in the Barbès neighbourhood of the capital, stone-throwing protesters burned Israeli flags: 'IsraHell', read one banner.

Only a year later, in 2015, in Paris once again, an attack occurred at a Hypercacher kosher supermarket in Porte de Vincennes in the wake of the Charlie Hebdo shooting two days earlier, and concurrently with the

Dammartin-en-Goële hostage crisis in which the two Charlie Hebdo gunmen were cornered.

The perpetrator, Amedy Coulibaly, had pledged allegiance to the Islamic State of Iraq and the Levant, and was a close friend of Saïd Kouachi and Chérif Kouachi, the gunmen in the Charlie Hebdo attack. Armed with a submachine gun, an assault rifle, and two Tokarev pistols, he entered and attacked the people in the kosher supermarket. Coulibaly murdered four Jewish hostages, and held fifteen other hostages during a siege in which he demanded that the Kouachi brothers not be harmed. The police ended the siege by storming the shop and killing Coulibaly. But that was not before Jewish institutions in the area had been placed under lockdown. The fear among Jews in the area grew considerably, and, despite shows of bravado in demonstrations, and many young non-Jewish people demonstrating in solidarity and wearing *Je suis Juif* 'I am a Jew' badges, the discomfort was there to stay, and Jews became ever more watchful.

It has taken several serious and violent attacks and murders to bring the government, in the shape of Manuel Valls, to a point where it will take antisemitism seriously. The contrast between the French unwillingness to name the antisemitism and the UK government's concern is a stark one. From denying the antisemitic nature of the abduction of Ilan Halimi to continuing to discuss social deprivation in the *banlieues*, it has been an unfocused and antisemitism-denying response.

Finally, the French government has begun to take some of this seriously. In February 2019, some of the *gilets jaunes* demonstrators began to attack Alain Finkielkraut, the distinguished French philosopher. The demonstrators could be heard shouting: 'Go back to Tel Aviv!', 'We are France!', 'Zionist! Big Zionist shit!' and 'France is ours!' on videos distributed on social media. Finkielkraut said that he 'sensed absolute hatred, and unfortunately it's not the first time,' and added that he 'would have been frightened if it had not been for the security forces'. Finkielkraut is the son of a Polish Auschwitz survivor and a vocal supporter of Israel, as well as a prominent intellectual. He had also shown some sympathy for the 'yellow vests' movement. President Macron denounced the antisemitic insults and called them 'the absolute negation of everything we are and what makes us a great nation. We will not tolerate them.'[94]

Just a couple of days later, ninety-six graves in a Jewish cemetery in Quatzenheim in eastern France were desecrated and defaced with swastikas. This looked like the work of the far-right. One grave was daubed with the words *Elsässischen Schwarzen Wölfe*, Alsatian Black Wolves, the name of the far-right group that campaigned for independence for Alsace in the 1970s. Once again, President Macron spoke out, and tens of thousands of people joined rallies against antisemitism the evening after the desecration. And a couple of weeks later, in Strasbourg, the memorial stone for the old synagogue burnt down by the Nazis in 1940 was vandalised. The combination in France of the rise of the far-right and the prevalence of Muslim antisemitism has led to a huge rise – 74 per cent – in antisemitic attacks in 2018 compared with the previous year.

There is clearly an issue in France, which explains why many French Jews are leaving. The Institute of Jewish Policy Research published research in early 2017 comparing recent trends of Jewish migration with cases of mass migration in response to persecution or major political upheavals in the past.[95]

The IJPR looked at six countries – France, Belgium, Germany, Italy, Sweden and the UK, which account for about 70 per cent of European Jews. It concluded there had been an increase in migration, especially from France, Belgium and Italy, but that in the UK, Germany and Sweden levels of migration were not unusual. The research showed 4 per cent of Jews in Belgium and France had left for Israel between 2010 and 2015, while the proportion leaving from the UK, Germany and Sweden was tiny by comparison, between 0.6 per cent and 1.7 per cent. Daniel Staetsky, author of the IJPR report, commented that 'European demographic and political landscapes are changing ... Large segments of Jewish populations in European countries perceive antisemitism to be on the increase.'[96]

There is, of course, no perfect way of measuring the prevalence and strength of antisemitic attitudes in the general public, but the perception, if not the reality, has led to some behaviour change. Jews often move, if they can, in response to an acute deterioration in their wellbeing and safety, so if Jews are beginning to feel unwelcome in Europe, the first sign of that will be some of them moving out.

And that is what we are beginning to see in parts of Europe. Although we have to be careful to acknowledge that the reasons may not wholly be related to antisemitism, it is clearly a major contributory factor.

One final example I would like to focus on here is the devastating mass shooting that took place in October 2018 at the Etz Chayyim synagogue in Squirrel Hill, Pittsburgh, USA. In scale, it was enormous. But it also has some strange messages, important for all right-thinking people to hear.

A gunman burst into the synagogue during a baby-naming ceremony on Saturday (the Sabbath), shouting 'all Jews must die' before killing eleven people and leaving six others wounded. The suspect had no criminal record and was unknown to the authorities. In later news coverage, contemporaries at school described him as shadowy, and said he was always full of hate. We know that he had left a trail of vile white supremacist comments and antisemitic abuse on social media, including sharing posts denying the Holocaust, but that gave no clue that he was capable of murder as well.

An hour before the attack, he wrote on the Gab social media forum, much criticised for providing an outlet for far-right figureheads and conspiracy theorists banned by other channels and social networks:[97] 'HIAS likes to bring invaders in that kill our people. I can't sit by and watch my people get slaughtered. Screw your optics, I'm going in.'

HIAS is what used to be called the Hebrew Immigrant Aid Society. It has helped Soviet Jews fleeing antisemitism in the former Soviet Union, poor Polish and Russian Jews in the early years of the twentieth century, Falash Mura (Ethiopian Jews), and many others, including those fleeing Nazi antisemitism and murderous intentions in 1930s Germany and Austria. According to Lev Golinkin, himself a refugee from Soviet antisemitism,

HIAS was what remained when the rest of your life

had disintegrated, when there was no money, no way to communicate, no going back. HIAS was what kept you tethered to the world when you became a ghost, but weren't yet ready to die.

But then there were no large numbers of Jews in need of resettlement:

It was other people who needed help: children fleeing gang violence in Central America, victims of wars in East Asia, and most of all, refugees from the wars in the Middle East – people who had endured horrors that make my family's experience seem like a luxury cruise in comparison.[98]

There was of course a great deal of argument about whether HIAS, a Jewish organisation, should devote its resources to helping Muslims. HIAS insisted it should, as Jewish organisations such as World Jewish Relief do in the UK. As Mark Hetfield, the president and chief executive of HIAS, explained: 'We decided to help, not because they are Jewish, but because we are Jewish.'[99]

The Hebrew Immigrant Aid Society became simply HIAS, to reflect the fact that it was no longer the case that about 90 per cent of its clients were Jewish. It is also the case that after Donald Trump became president, HIAS became one of the most vigorous and vocal opponents of the White House's attempts to ban refugees.

After the Pittsburgh massacre, President Donald Trump, responding to questions about the availability of weapons to the gunman, was quick to insist that tougher gun laws – which many members of the Pittsburgh community supported – would have made little difference.

That is unlikely to be true, though it is clear that security guards at the entrance to the synagogue might well have made a difference. But there is no doubt that this latest attack will fuel fears that religious and racial hatred is on the rise during a fraught period of divisive politics. If the attacker in Pittsburgh was not only motivated by antisemitism but also by the role the Jewish community in America plays in fostering an open and equal society in which refugees can find welcome and haven, we can see where the problems might lie. The social divides are growing. This is where an antisemitic attack becomes more than just that. It is both antisemitic and Islamophobic. It points to something else: a level of intolerance and hatred that is allowed to fester, and is even encouraged by an official anti-immigration rhetoric.

After the massacre, President Trump said, as so many leaders have said before him, that 'This evil anti-Semitic attack is an assault on all of us.' But he continued by vowing to fully enforce the death penalty for such crimes. 'We must stand with our Jewish brothers and sisters to defeat anti-Semitism and vanquish the forces of hate.' In an increasingly polarised United States, Trump's words sounded pretty thin. The alleged gunman's views included complaining that President Donald Trump was surrounded by too many Jewish advisers and that the Jews were responsible for the caravan of Central American migrants heading toward the US–Mexico border. Basically, Jews are the cause of all white people's ills.

These white genocide conspiracy theories among antisemites are growing in popularity, even though they date back to the late nineteenth century, as discussed above. The Gab website was largely offline after the massacre, as various providers – PayPal, GoDaddy and others – refused to allow it to use their platforms. On the subject of conspiracy theories, there was much media discussion. AlterNet's Jacob Sugarman spoke with *New York Times* reporter Jonathan Weisman in April 2018:

> When white nationalists talk about so-called white genocide, they imagine that white human beings, specifically white men, are being supplanted and driven out by brown people: African-Americans, Latinos, Muslims and immigrants more generally . . . But their mythology also tells them that these brown people are inferior beings, so they summon the Jews as the cause of their demise, the answer to the question, 'How could this be happening to us?' It's the Jews, they believe, who are the puppet masters, pulling the strings of the ethnic hordes. You can't separate one group from another, we're all in this together.[100]

There's a final ironic twist to this appalling story. Ari Mahler, the nurse looking after the alleged attacker and murderer, Robert Bowers, was Jewish. On the Saturday night after the massacre, Mahler put up a Facebook post that went viral:

> I am The Jewish Nurse. Yes, that Jewish Nurse. The same one that people are talking about in the Pittsburgh shooting that left 11 dead. The trauma nurse in the ER that cared for Robert Bowers who yelled, 'Death to all Jews,' as he was wheeled into the hospital. The Jewish nurse who ran into a room to save his life . . . To be honest, I'm nervous about sharing this, I just know I feel alone right now and the irony of the world talking

about me doesn't seem fair without the chance to speak for myself.

Mahler was one of three Jewish doctors and nurses to tend to Bowers when he was brought to Allegheny General Hospital with gunshot wounds sustained during a shoot-out with police. The son of a rabbi, Mahler noted that he 'experienced anti-Semitism a lot' as a kid, including swastikas drawn on his locker and pictures drawn showing him and his family being marched to a gas chamber. 'The fact that I did my job, a job which requires compassion and empathy over everything, is newsworthy because I'm Jewish. Even more so because my dad's a Rabbi.' He said that Bowers 'thanked him for saving him, for showing him kindness and for treating him the same way I treat every other patient.' Mahler said that he did not tell Bowers that he was Jewish. 'I chose not to say anything the entire time. I wanted him to feel compassion. I chose to show him empathy. I felt that the best way to honor his victims was for a Jew to prove him wrong.'[101]

From Denmark to Belgium, from Italy to the United States, there are growing numbers of attacks – too many for me to cite them all. Each is different, of course. But the hatred appears to be growing, and it is curiously confused. It ranges from rage about the Middle East and a 'defence of the Palestinians', to a sense that Jews hold too much power and are responsible, in some unspecified way, for encouraging more immigrants into the country. It is about an attack on those who threaten white men – and it is largely, though not entirely, male. It is about arguing that Hitler was right, that Jews are a plague within European society. The cancer analogy is not as far-fetched as it may seem. To Jews, it appears that the cancer remission has ended, and what had been isolated symptoms reappearing is now developing into a general experience of the disease. For the antisemites, it seems that the strong antidote given, which allowed Jews to flourish once again in Europe, is coming to an end, and that the Jews themselves are the cancer, the cause of the general malaise. In Denmark particularly, the official response has been rapid and wholly supportive of the Jewish community. In other countries, it has often been more muted, and some commentators have even argued that official anti-immigrant rhetoric has fanned the flames of this new born antisemitism.

This phenomenon is still playing out, but the concern remains among many Jews that anti-immigrant rhetoric affects their position considerably, as it does for Muslims, and that it can no longer be ignored.

CHAPTER 3

How does it feel?

In a word, uncomfortable. The long-held post-Second World War sense of security, that has spanned all my adult life and that of my children, is still there. But it has been dented. Britain is still a good place to be Jewish, and Jewish communal activities are flourishing. It is markedly different to be Jewish in London now from when I grew up in the 1950s and 1960s; we have a brilliant UK Jewish Film Festival, Jewish Book Week is now a significant event on the literary calendar, we have a large Jewish Community Centre in the shape of JW3 in Hampstead, plus music events, debates and sporting competitions and much more. All signs of a thriving, confident community.

But it is also a more worried, somewhat uneasy community. It was an extraordinary decision for the Jewish community to organise a demonstration against antisemitism in the Labour party in Parliament Square in March 2018, at which I was present.[1] But there were positives in that. For at that rally, various Labour MPs, Jewish and non-Jewish alike, spoke alongside Jewish community leaders, and other minority groups, including Muslims, Sikhs and Catholics, lent their support and encouragement. Only the presence of Corbyn-supporting Labour members taking photographs of any Labour

MPs and peers attending gave it an uneasy feel. It was highly charged emotionally, and was followed by all three main Jewish communal newspapers sharing the headline 'United we stand', warning that a Jeremy Corbyn-led government would pose an 'existential threat to Jewish life'. It was hard to believe that this could happen in my staid, secure, Jewish community. But people were asking themselves whether Jeremy Corbyn would have treated any other minority community complaining of discrimination and racism with such contempt.

Equally, the rise of open intolerance on the right of the political spectrum – the appointment of Tommy Robinson as an adviser to the leader of UKIP, open Islamophobic statements by many, and Conservative MP Suella Braverman's use of the term 'cultural Marxism', albeit innocently on her part, are all causes for concern. She did not understand it – though she should have done – but 'cultural Marxism' was a term used by the Norwegian far-right activist and mass murderer Anders Breivik and others, and dates back largely to the Nazis. They capitalised on the strong feeling 'that there had been a cultural and moral collapse in Germany prior to 1933':

> *Kulturbolschewismus* (cultural bolshevism) and Jewish bolshevism were used as explanations by the Nazis for a supposed plot to spread sexual, political (communist) and other revolution throughout the Weimar Republic and the west, and to weaken and attack German culture as part of a wider international conspiracy. This idea, building on *Mein Kampf* and the anti-Semitic Protocols of the Elders of Zion, has survived, developed, and is now used to suggest that . . . Jewish people, other minority

communities, or anyone with progressive beliefs are, as communist sympathisers, conspiring through media and academic domination to implement cultural Marxism and undermine western culture or Christian values.[2]

Each of these events is small in itself, but the increasing anti-migrant feeling, and the intolerance and anger surrounding the Brexit debate, has had its effect. Though most British Jews have had generations of history in the UK, we were partly caught up in the crossfire.

And then came the attack on the synagogue in Pittsburgh. It shocked the community in Britain, for its horror of course, but also for what it showed could happen as a result of a right-wing conspiracy theory that blames the Jews for everything, including for Muslims being allowed to immigrate into the United States. Comfort came from those non-Jews, many Muslims among them, who stood up for the Jewish community in the aftermath and at the memorials, but the shock and hurt remain nevertheless, and the complacent sense of security has been further dented.

Solidarity

Hearing of the abuse that has to be endured by those who stand up to antisemitism has also increased the concern. As I was finishing work on this book, Rachel Riley, presenter on the popular game show *Countdown* on Channel 4, took a brave and public aim at the antisemites supporting Labour:

> In the name of Labour, I've been called a hypocrite, lying propagandist, teeth, tits and ass, clothes-horse

dolly-bird, weaponiser of antisemitism, fascist, right-wing extremist, Nazi sympathiser, Twitter-cancer, thick, Tory, brainwashed, an antisemite, white-supremacist, Zio-political trollster, not a real Jew, a child bully, bonkers mad conspiracy theorist, a paedo-protector minion puppet whom my dead grandfather would be disgusted by. After I used the recent anniversary of my 10 years as *Countdown*'s numbers lady as an opportunity to give this topic a bigger platform, with an on-camera interview, an 11,500 word article was written with the sole intention of discrediting many brave and dedicated people standing up to antisemitism. I can only describe this article as A-grade conspiracy garbage, complete with go-to clips, neo-Nazi like, to use to 'prove' that 'antisemitism's just a trick'. A quarter of the article was about me, including how I'm antisemitic and should be fired.[3]

This made the national news, and Riley received enormous support from her Twitter followers and the wider world.[4] There is real comfort from this. The Jewish community is feeling increasingly disturbed by the antisemitic attitudes it is encountering from left and right alike. But it celebrates and appreciates those who stand alongside, those who call out the antisemitism wherever it occurs, and those who shared in the 'Enough is enough' demonstration in Parliament Square in March 2018. The fact that the Royal Mint shelved plans to issue a commemorative coin in 2014 to mark the centenary since Roald Dahl's birth was much welcomed. Dahl, beloved for his children's books, became an ardent and self-confessed antisemite in his later years, and is famous for saying: 'There is a trait in the Jewish character that does provoke animosity, maybe it's a kind of lack of generosity towards non-Jews . . . There is always a reason why anti-anything crops up anywhere; even a stinker like Hitler didn't just pick on them for no reason.'[5]

Added to this is the enormous support from many churches and mosques, the wonderful sight of Muslim women wearing skullcaps over their hijabs during a demonstration to protest against an antisemitic attack in Berlin in 2018, solidarity demonstrations in Paris and throughout Germany, and much more. Many people and institutions are expressing solidarity, and, more than that, real friendship. It was wonderful to see, after the Pittsburgh massacre, the Muslim Home Secretary, Sajid Javid, and the Muslim Mayor of London, Sadiq Khan, standing shoulder to shoulder with Jews in London, as did a whole variety of Muslim organisations, from the Muslim Council of Britain to Tell MAMA, an organisation that monitors Islamophobia and supports victims of anti-Muslim hatred. The considerable fellow feeling between many Muslims and Jews was, and is, constantly expressed. Muslims too form a minority group in UK society, and they, and we, know that attacks do not remain focused against only one group.

Hearing people who are not Jewish call out right-wing conspiracy theorists and those whose shadowy views seem to be moving towards a belief in white supremacy brings a sense that things may change, and these views may be pushed back to where they were before. Unsayable. Unthinkable. Unacceptable in polite society. And just plain wrong.

And Yet . . .

Nevertheless, the unease is growing. Well-integrated British Jews have been feeling the pinch throughout this decade. It has been exacerbated by a variety of factors, from what has gone on in the Labour party to the physical attacks on Jews in Europe, from increasing numbers of antisemitic incidents in the UK to, more recently, the Pittsburgh massacre, right in the heart of what we have always thought of as safe space for Jews, the United States, where the far-right gathered in Charlottesville in 2017 for what became a shameful white supremacist rally and were heard shouting 'Jews will not replace us'.[6]

High-profile journalists have gone public about the serious issues we are facing as Jews. Hugo Rifkind, columnist for *The Times*, reported feeling 'exposed' as a Jew in an article in August 2014.[7] Daniel Finkelstein displayed his anger,[8] while David Aaronovitch, Jonathan Freedland, the historian Simon Sebag Montefiore – who suggested he was thinking of leaving the UK[9] – and others all did likewise. They may have had different things to say about their views, and all had different experiences to share, but one thing was clear – a change in the music was, and is, palpable.

We can see and hear antisemitic chants and placards at pro-Palestinian rallies. The word 'Yid' is shouted endlessly at Spurs football matches, but is no longer in itself an arrestable offence, despite being highly offensive and derogatory.[10] Antisemitic incidents are growing in number, with the 2018 figures showing a 16 per cent increase on previous years. Antisemitic incident numbers usually 'spike' when there is a war in the Middle East involving Israel. This 2018 spike came when there was no such war.

There were also disputes about the facts of antisemitism. In January 2015, newspaper headlines around the world reported that nearly half of Britons subscribed to at least one antisemitic belief. Those headlines were based on the findings of a YouGov survey commissioned by the Campaign against Antisemitism. Yet again, my American friends were calling and emailing and asking me if I felt safe in Britain. And, yet again, I had to say I felt totally safe, and if they were worried about antisemitism, they should look at France.

What was not reported was that the CAA's report also attracted serious criticism from more established Jewish organisations, many of whom were reportedly 'absolutely furious' with its unprofessional use of survey techniques. Anshel Pfeffer, a veteran reporter for the Israeli newspaper *Ha'aretz*, argued that several of the allegedly antisemitic beliefs polled by YouGov in their survey do not necessarily amount to antisemitism, and he criticised the methodology of CAA's survey of British Jews as leading to an unrepresentative sample. He added:

> The last finding in the survey is that 56 per cent agree that 'the recent rise in anti-Semitism in Britain has some echoes of the 1930s'. If the majority of British Jews and the authors of the CAA report actually believe that, then it's hard to take anything they say about contemporary anti-Semitism in their home country seriously. If they honestly think that the situation in Britain today echoes the 1930s . . . when a popular fascist party, supported by members of the nobility and popular newspapers, were

marching in support of Hitler, when large parts of the British establishment were appeasing Nazi Germany and the government was resolutely opposed to allowing Jewish refugees of Nazism in to Britain ... and when the situation of Jews in other European countries at the time was so much worse, then not only are they woefully ignorant of recent Jewish history but have little concept of what real anti-Semitism is beyond the type they see online.[11]

This is the point precisely. Yes, there is antisemitism, but it is not like the 1930s – it is nowhere near – and when members of the UK Jewish community react hysterically, as a few have, it is important to bring them back down to earth.

Jonathan Boyd, executive director of the Institute for Jewish Policy Research (JPR), dismissed CAA's survey as having 'little, if any, methodological credibility'. He argued that a far more accurate and honest reading of the data would highlight the fact that between 75 per cent and 90 per cent of people in Britain either do not hold antisemitic views or have no particular view of Jews either way. Only about 4 per cent to 5 per cent of people can be characterised as clearly antisemitic when looking at individual measures of antisemitism. Not great, but not so terrible either. And the deputy director of the Community Security Trust, Mark Gardner, emphasised, rightly, that 'most of the time, most British Jews do not encounter antisemitism and are able to live whatever Jewish lives they choose'.

How it feels ought to depend on the facts. Accurate work such as that by CST/JPR is cautious and rigorous, and that is why it needs to be taken seriously. It should also give the Jewish community a certain amount of comfort. Daniel Staetsky's 2017 study of antisemitism in contemporary Britain gives a much more nuanced picture than the CAA survey.[12] For instance, it found that only a small proportion of British adults can be categorised as 'hard-core' antisemites – approximately 2 per cent. But it goes on to explain that antisemitic ideas can be found at varying degrees of intensity across 30 per cent of British society. It is that 'echo chamber of ideas' that Jews in Britain have probably been picking up. It clearly does not mean that 30 per cent of the British population is antisemitic, but 'it does demonstrate the outer boundary of the extent to which antisemitic ideas live and breathe in British society'. That research also, rightly, introduced the concept of the 'elastic view' of antisemitism,[13] arguing that as antisemitism is an attitude it is bound to exist at different scales and levels of intensity. That is why no single figure can capture the accurate level of antisemitism in society. Any figures cited need to be carefully explained and understood, and viewed with caution. It is not simple – how we feel about it all cannot be simple either.

The complexity of the Jewish reactions to all this is exacerbated by the extent to which this is about Israel as well as simply about Jews. That same research also found that levels of attitudes hostile to Israel, so-called anti-Israelism, are considerably higher than levels of anti-Jewish feeling, and that the two attitudes exist both independently of one another and together. But the greater the intensity of an anti-Israel attitude, the more likely it is to be accompanied by antisemitic attitudes, a point well made in Dave Rich's *The Left's Jewish Problem*.[14] Rich, CST's Head of Policy, analyses what has happened as the Labour party has gradually and now more substantively been taken over by the hard-left, and looks at how views we once thought were fringe and fanatical – conspiracy theories, old antisemitic canards – are now the preserve of 'right-thinking leftists'. Nick Cohen, reviewing Rich's book, went even further:

> If Rich has a fault, it is that as a rational historian, he cannot speculate on the psychological appeal of left antisemitism. Novelists would notice the attraction of an authorised racism to leftists, who in other respects are highly constrained in what they can say by speech codes. They would find that a prejudice that endorsed fascism as well as 2,000 years of Christian polemics and persecutions fitted far-left political beliefs rather well. It is not a large step, after all, to go from saying that democracy is a swindle perpetrated by the 'neoliberal' world order, to saying that the swindlers are the 'Rothschilds', the 'Zionists', the – oh, let's just spit it out – the Jews.[15]

For the Jewish community, rattled by growing evidence of antisemitism and finding it hard to come to terms with it, the evidence the JPR report uncovered by looking at different groups of the population was of paramount importance. Levels of antisemitism and anti-Israelism among Christians are no different from those found across society as a whole. Among Muslims, they are somewhat higher on both counts. But on the political spectrum, levels of antisemitism are found to be clearly the highest among the far-right, and levels of anti-Israelism are heightened across all parts of the left, but particularly on the far-left. In all cases, the higher the level of anti-Israelism, the more likely it is to be accompanied by antisemitism. Yet what was important was the conclusion that most of the antisemitism found in British society exists *outside* these three groups – the far-left, far-right and Muslims; even at its most heightened levels of intensity, only about 15 per cent of it can be accounted for by them. It is a cancer within society at large, even if not at enormously high levels.

This makes for uncomfortable, yet hardly alarming, reading. Yet the response to it, by those who shout about it loudest, is to say that many Jews are thinking of packing their bags and leaving Britain. There is no real evidence to suggest a third of British Jews are seriously thinking of leaving, as some have declared. There is no evidence at all that this is like the 1930s. Yet it is true to say that the Friday night dinner table conversation has changed. People are talking about what would make them leave Britain altogether, which simply was not the case before around the year 2000, when there was a surge in antisemitism after the second Intifada. And that is important, because it does reflect insecurity, even if few have actually left.

The EU's Fundamental Rights Agency Report on discrimination and hate crime against Jews published as long ago as 2013 showed that 1 per cent of UK respondents 'did emigrate but have returned' and 18 per cent 'have considered emigrating', when giving an answer to 'views about emigrating from country because of not feeling safe living there as a Jew, in the past five years'. French figures at that time were 3 per cent and 46 per cent respectively. But, by 2018, the FRA report shows the UK figure now at 1 per cent and 29 per cent respectively, whereas France is at 2 per cent and 44 per cent respectively. So the UK figures have worsened, while France, usually considered the most antisemitic country in Western Europe, has stayed static.[16]

At Jewish New Year in September 2018, Hadley Freeman commented in her *Guardian* column: 'It's Jewish New Year, a time to eat and talk – and there'll only be one topic at the table. As I dip my apple slice in honey, I will think about the days when Jews were not fretting about antisemitism going mainstream in Britain.'[17] The mood music has changed, and it is that change which British Jews are picking up. At first, all this means is a sense of unease, almost unspoken, alongside the shouting and screaming and frequent overreaction. It also leads many Jews who identified with the left and the hard-left to question their former friends and allies, and react in horror. Curiously, it also leads to more of those erstwhile left sympathisers becoming more consciously Jewish, determined to 'rescue' something in themselves they had hitherto ignored, but which is now causing them such pain because others – former colleagues and allies in the fight against capitalism, and the campaign for equality – are despising them for it and disregarding their views on other matters because they are Jews. There is a sense of aggravated fear within the Jewish community, an increasing super-sensitivity to mild remarks, and also, worryingly, an increasing likelihood of seeing antisemitism where it does not exist. Abigail Morris, director of the Jewish Museum in Camden, puts the situation well, with the tension between over-sensitivity and outsiders feeling that the community must be over-reacting, and the lived experience: 'People think we're making a fuss; they see a settled, wealthy, high-achieving community. They don't understand that, within our parents' and grandparents' lifetimes, it was all destroyed.'[18]

More fundamentally, for the older generation who remember the post-war years in the fifties, sixties and seventies, there is a sad and resigned recognition that the oldest hatred hasn't gone away. And for younger Jews, who have spent their formative years going about their business thinking themselves truly accepted and simply Jewish by ethnic identity – whether that relates to peoplehood or religion – it has come as a great shock. Suddenly, they feel they are 'the other'. They recognise what Tony Blair was saying when he warned of Jew hate taking root in British society: 'too often, we have seen how anti-Zionism trends easily into antisemitism. The scourge that we fought to eradicate in the twentieth century has been allowed to make a comeback.'[19] For the first time, they feel objectified, as non-Jewish work colleagues and friends ask them, as if they are an object of curiosity, whether there really *is* antisemitism in the Labour party or in society more generally, or whether somehow this isn't all an exaggeration. Was the Pittsburgh murderer really an antisemitic white supremacist, whose views are shared by many others, or was he just mentally deranged? I always advise those who ask that question, unpalatable though it is, to check the Gab website and others, and look at what the alt-right in the United States is putting out in terms of fake news and licensed xenophobia. Young Jews talk of feeling both objectified and somehow the lightning rod for judging whether antisemitism really exists and is growing. This generation, largely only moderately participative in

Jewish life in the UK up to now, are returning to their synagogues and Jewish organisations in their droves. Their Jewish consciousness has been awakened by some of this. How sad that it should take antisemitism to do it. And their identity – as they have perceived it thus far – has been profoundly threatened.

And there is anger – anger that such idiotic claims about Jews are allowed to circulate, anger that people believe them, anger at the level of vitriol and hatred being spread about Jewish women Labour MPs, anger at the nature of discussion on university campuses, anger that swastikas can be openly shown on flags at anti-Israel demonstrations, anger at the violent antisemitic attacks in Europe and fear that they will one day spread to the UK. That anger extends to the attacks on Israel and the holding of Israel to impossible standards in the British media.

And there is real concern that things will get worse. Despite the facts, despite the known experience that the UK is still one of the safest and happiest places in the world to be a Jew, insecurity is rising.

But there is something else. Alongside all this, there is a canary-in-the-mine fear, which takes the argument wider than the Jews. First comes the question of whether Muslims will get the same treatment too, when it seems as if they might from reading the works of white Christian supremacists, who attack both Jews and Muslims in equal measure. That is one good reason for Jews and Muslims to make common cause, as they are beginning to do. And there seem to be some examples of anti-Muslim incidents in the Labour party, as well as among Conservatives, which strengthen that argument.[20] So Jews are not alone.

But the anti-racism movement, behind which the hard-left tends to hide, is not seen, and largely never has been, as protecting Jews. This may be because Jews are largely, with exceptions, white. The antiracism of the sixties, seventies and eighties was about racism against people who were black, about those from the Caribbean and those from East Africa. Despite the fact that Jews and Poles, among others, are now clearly targeted for abuse, anti-racists still do not include Jews among the people whom racism affects – they cannot, or choose not to, see the problem. It may be because Jews are seen as 'privileged', part of the 'elite' who cause the suffering experienced by the dispossessed poor. Because Jews are seen as clever, able to surmount any prejudice, any barriers, placed in their way – part of the old trope about Jews' fiendish intelligence. It may be because – according to antisemitic canards – Jews will always band together, and therefore defeat any obstacles. It may be because – according to this appalling line of thinking – Jews have 'overplayed' the effect on the Jewish community of the Holocaust. Whatever the reasons, Jews are not included in, and do not fit into, the antiracism rhetoric of the far-left.

And this is where the canary-in-the-mine argument matters. If it is possible, while self-identifying as an antiracist, to hold vile views about Jews, to believe untruths, to regard Jews as not properly British, to conflate Jews and Israel, and to see them as benighted capitalists and a troubling elite, and *still* say you're an antiracist, there is a gas seeping out that will eventually kill you all. The line simply will not withstand close examination. You cannot, with intellectual honesty, claim to be an antiracist and say Jews have no sense of irony. You cannot, as an antiracist, fail to see the caricaturing of the Jews as capitalists grinding the faces of the poor as deeply prejudiced and unfair. You cannot conflate Israel and Jews, and allow the name-calling of Jewish students as Zio and not feel it as a body blow. If you cannot see or feel these things, then you are a racist – because you have not accepted that antisemitism is as racist, if different in tone, as the racism against Muslims, Sikhs, Hindus and people of Afro-Caribbean heritage.

And the converse applies on the right. You cannot use the words 'cosmopolitan' and 'money power' as coded references to Jews and think you won't be rumbled. You cannot use the words 'north London metropolitan elite' as a code term for Jewish, as *The Times* did of Danny Cohen, then the BBC's director of television, after he fired Jeremy Clarkson.[21] You cannot point out, as the *Daily Mail* did, that Ralph Miliband, father of David and Ed, was a refugee from Nazism and then carry on by suggesting his allegiance was to Moscow, that he was one of those 'rootless cosmopolitans'.[22]

There was a famous conversation at Jewish Book Week in London in 2007 between Martin Amis, who recalled his father's polite antisemitism, and Christopher Hitchens, who had discovered he was a Jew on his mother's side – she had concealed it – in the 1970s, and realised that his father had partly Jewish antecedents. His attitude to that discovery is fascinating. It made him identify as a Jew, despite his militant atheism:

> If my mother's intention in whole or in part was to ensure that I never had to suffer any indignity or embarrassment for being a Jew, then she succeeded well enough. And in

any case there were enough intermarriages and 'conversions' on both sides of her line to make me one of those many mischling hybrids who are to be found distributed all over the known world. And, as someone who doesn't really believe that the human species is subdivided by 'race', let alone that a nation or nationality can be defined by its religion, why should I not let the whole question slide away from me? Why – and then I'll stop asking rhetorical questions – did I at some point resolve that, in whatever tone of voice I was asked 'Are you a Jew?' I would never hear myself deny it?[23]

In that conversation, Amis and Hitchens nailed the danger of antisemitism, and I could not have put it better:

Antisemitism is a very, very serious cultural danger, and it's only a fool who thinks that it is a threat only to Jews. Antisemitism is a very, very toxic threat to everything we can decently call 'civilization' . . . If someone says they don't like West Indians, because of their – I don't know what it might be – their music. Or they don't like Indians because of the smell of their cooking. Or they don't like Koreans for their kimchi – whatever it might be. Every minority and majority in the world has a version of this kind of prejudice . . . But, as Freud pointed out, they'll all sink their differences when it comes to the Jews. And with the Jews it's not their cooking or their sex lives or any of this, and it's not just vulgar prejudice about skin colour or smell. It's a theory. It's a paranoid theory that tries to explain quite a lot. It's fascinated with gold, with secret documents, with missing codices in ancient treaties, with the idea of an invisible and secret government . . . And it affects both left and right . . . It is becoming normal. And it sits in a world of fake news and social media, where, if you repeat something often enough, people begin to believe it.[24]

Vasily Grossman, the Ukrainian Jewish author, had it right when he suggested in his 1960 masterpiece *Life and Fate*[25] that antisemitism is like a vast mirror, an ocean of insecurities. For some reason, people – ordinary people – seem to be able to gravitate towards the Jew as the explanation of and reason for all their frustrations. Pair that with social media and fake news reinforcing all sorts of nonsense, and you have a pretty lethal cocktail. So you can think on the one hand that Jews are contemptible, or not quite British, or have dual loyalties, or smell, but you can also think that they are mega powerful, part of an international conspiracy against you, too rich and successful. And you can think all those things at once.

It is indeed a theory. It's truly a paranoid theory. It waxes and wanes, but sometimes it catches fire. It is at a low level as yet in the UK, but its flames are being fanned by the far-left and the far-right, even by those who claim to be antiracists. A good analogy is that of a serious house fire. We all know intellectually that houses do catch fire, but most of the time the danger is remote, and a house, one's home, is a place of security and safety, a refuge from anything frightening outside. A serious fire in your own home, your safe space, reminds you of the fragility of that security, the terrifying capability of the structures to sustain a destructive conflagration. You realise that houses burning down, including your own house, is not just something that used to happen but is an ever-present danger throughout human history. The present insecurity among the UK's Jewish population is like that: the Labour party's reluctance to deal with antisemitism, the rise of crude antisemitism openly expressed on the right, the prevalence of antisemitism in some extreme Muslim publications – all this reminds us of the fragility of our stability. What we used to interpret as the loony theories of crazy auto-didacts now appear to be part of an ancient narrative that links disasters of the past to dangers in the future. And, at the edges of those paranoid, loony theories, the tropes that go with them are beginning to be seen and heard among those who hitherto did not have an antisemitic bone in their bodies. Because this stuff spreads.

That's why it matters. It matters because it smells, it rots the body politic, it leads to worse, and it renders rational thought incapable in the face of an ineluctable, active theory of why 'they' are to blame. It destroys normal, rational, evidenced-based thought. It matters – to Jews and non-Jews alike. And it links up with an anti-elitist wave that is sweeping Western Europe and the United States, though not all Jews are part of the elite by any means. This becomes a way of justifying an age-old prejudice and hatred in new-fangled garb; it's not because they are Jews we hate them, but because they are part of the elite, in the media, the banks, the universities, the judiciary, medicine – you name it, they've clawed their way to the top.

But there is still some room for optimism. Polling shows that most people either know that Labour has an antisemitism problem or that they don't know anything about Jews or antisemitism but still think badly of Labour because of it. There has been outrage at antisemitism from left and right among many hundreds of thousands of decent people. But I still feel uneasy. I feel uneasy as a Jew, having felt secure as a proud British subject all my life, with a strong sense of gratitude to the UK for taking in my mother and grandparents in the 1930s. I feel uneasy as a British subject, thinking how what starts with this might spread and affect other minorities, most of whom have been proudly and openly supportive of the Jewish community through all this. I do not want to live in a country where intolerance and hatred become the norm. I do not want Brexit to have fractured our accepting and tolerant way of life in Britain. And I do not want to believe that it might be possible to echo that great German Protestant pastor Martin Niemoeller, who wrote in 1946, as a committed anti-Nazi who narrowly escaped execution and spent time in concentration camps between 1938 and 1945:

> First they came for the socialists, and I did not speak out –
> Because I was not a socialist.
> Then they came for the trade unionists, and I did not speak out –
> Because I was not a trade unionist.
> Then they came for the Jews, and I did not speak out –
> Because I was not a Jew.
> Then they came for me – and there was no one left to speak for me.[26]

This is not only about Jews. If this is what is being said about Jews, what will be said about Muslims, Hindus or Jains? And some of it already is. What will be said about black people, gay people and disabled people? About anyone who is not part of what people want to see as the 'true' British people? And that's why we should be wary and keep a keen eye, on left and right alike, and on the unformed middle, and watch for the spread of hatred, and call it out.

I am still comforted by my optimistic and passionate belief in the fairmindedness of my country, and of the British people. Despite the nagging insecurity, I hope and believe that the British people will see all this off as the foul and irrational hatred that it is. I hope and believe that this vile smell of antisemitism, along with Islamophobia, other racism and intolerance, will be packed back up in the stinking bags where it belongs, and rendered once again both unsayable and unacceptable. And I hope that by looking at antisemitism in the face, discussing it and teasing out the nuances, people will understand why Jews are uneasy, and support them in the fight against it – for the sake of all of us who want to live in a tolerant, open, accepting, democratic society.

ACKNOWLEDGEMENTS

This book has been long in the gestation and there are so many people to thank that naming a few seems invidious. But some have gone far beyond the call of duty, in particular: Jenny Lord, my amazing editor and publisher at Weidenfeld & Nicolson, who has been a support and firm guide throughout. Steve Rubin, publisher and friend extraordinaire, who was the midwife of this project, and made sure it happened – I can never thank him enough. Leanne Oliver, for all her work making sure the book got noticed, and Holly Harley, John English, Simon Wright and Kate Shearman for all their work on copy-editing and spotting mistakes. David Byrne SC whose questions over dinner in Ireland in summer 2018 got me started on some of the tricky issues in this book. The late Sir Peter Sutherland who always told me I needed to write a book about this, and would have added more material about the Roman Catholic Church. The Right Reverend Lord Harries of Pentregarth, for many questions and so much support, in so many ways. Lord Wilson of Tillyorn, and his wife Natasha, for even more questions and comments on many walks. The Very Reverend Dr John Hall, Dean of Westminster Abbey, for his support and friendship. Mark Gardner, deputy director of the Community Security Trust and Head of Communications, who read through much of the first version and was a helpful guide. Dave Rich, Policy Director at CST, who did much of the same. Jon Boyd, Chief Executive, Institute for Jewish Policy

Research, for making detailed comments on the book's outline. Thomas Harding, for some rigorous criticism and hugely helpful suggestions. Stephen Moss CBE for telling me not to believe the hype! Lord Mitchell for his advice and comments about how it feels to him. Baroness Royall of Blaisdon for her courage and support. Jim Fletcher for encouraging me and feeding me material. Imam Monawar Hussain, founder of the Oxford Foundation, for his courage and support. My friends Victoria Neumark, Katie Petty-Saphon and Joanna Waley-Cohen for questions and support, my aunt Anne Schwab, always there to give advice and always such a friend, and my beloved and late lamented colleague, Rabbi Harry Jacobi MBE, who died as the proofs of this book were being finalised. My rabbinic colleagues at West London Synagogue, Rabbis Helen Freeman, Neil Janes, David Mitchell and Sybil Sheridan, for everything. Chris and Deirdre Bowers-Broadbent, whose dinner party in February 2019 made me realise how to end the book. Paola Churchill, who keeps me in order and has done for twenty-five years, and crucially made sure I found a way to write this book. My family – Anthony, Harriet and Matthew, along with Claire and Aisling – you've listened to so much of this. My book group and my friends in London and Ireland – you've all been wonderful.

This book is dedicated to the memory of George Weidenfeld, founder of Weidenfeld & Nicolson, and my grandmother Anna Schwab. George always told me it was my grandmother's encouragement that really set him out on his amazing career, when she was chair of the welfare committee of the Refugee Committee in the 1930s, and he was a newly arrived refugee. He never forgot.

BIBLIOGRAPHY

David Aaronovitch, 'The new anti-Semitism. A document once used by the Nazis to stir up hatred of Jews and long known to be a forgery is once again being circulated, this time by Muslim scholars', *Observer*, 22 June 2003

Jonathan Adelman, 'The Christians of Israel: A Remarkable Group', HuffPost, 28 August 2015 (updated 28 August 2016)

Ofer Aderet, 'Anti-Semitism Growing Among Far Right and Muslim Migrants in Germany, State Premier Tells Haaretz', *Ha'aretz*, 3 September 2018

AFP news.france@thelocal.com, 'Why 5000 Jews emigrated from France to Israel last year', AFP, 9 January 2017, https://www.thelocal.fr/20170109/5000-more-jews-leave-france-for-israel

Algemeiner staff, 'Jewish Owned Stores Burned to the Ground, Synagogue Firebombed in "Paris Intifada"', *Algemeiner*, 21 July 2014

Aftab Ali, 'Oxford University Labour Club students did engage in anti-Semitic behaviour, report finds', *Independent*, 3 August 2016; Marcus Dysch, 'Baroness Royall report reveals Oxford Labour students engaged in antisemitism', *Jewish Chronicle*, 3 August 2016

Rod Ardehali, '"I can't thank people enough for seeing through the lies": *Countdown*'s Rachel Riley praises fans for their support after slamming Corbyn and telling George Galloway to f*** off in anti-Semitism row', Mailonline, 10 January 2019

Salo Wittmayer Baron, *A Social and Religious History of the Jews* (18 vols) (Columbia: Columbia University Press, 1952–1983)

Raymond Barre, *'Je l'avais connu et que c'était un homme bien'* – 'I knew him and he was a good man', *'L'antisémitisme ordinaire ou les dérapages de Raymond Barre'*, Zapping radio, 13 March 2007

Liz Bates and Kevin Schofield, 'Labour councillor suspended over "Jews drink blood and rape children" social media post', *PoliticsHome*, 27 July 2018

BBC News, 'Palestinians evicted in Jerusalem', 2 August 2009

___, 'Nazi stag-do Tory MP Aidan Burley to step down', 5 February 2014

Ian Black, 'Doctor admits Israeli pathologists harvested organs without consent', *Guardian*, 21 December 2009

Aurora Bosotti, 'Polling guru says Corbyn "under pressure" as Labour vote flop leaves party "empty handed"', *Express*, 5 May 2018

Donald Boström, '"Our sons are plundered of their organs" – Palestinians accuse the Israel Defense Forces of taking organs from their victims', *Aftonbladet*, 26 August 2009

Jonathan Boyd, Researching antisemitism, Institute for Jewish Policy Research, London, 14 January 2015

Lizzy Buchan, 'Tory MEPs ordered to distance themselves from Hungary's far-right Viktor Orbán after vote controversy', *Independent*, 13 September 2018

James Carroll, 'One Cardinal's Old Impulse to Blame Jews', *Boston Globe*, 13 August 2003

Louis-Ferdinand Céline (Ralph Manheim trs.), *Journey to the End of the Night* (Richmond: Alma Classics, 2012)

Levon Chorbajian and George Shirinian (eds.), *Studies in Comparative Genocide* (Basingstoke: Palgrave Macmillan, 1999)

David Clegg, 'Labour suspend councillor over claims he told Anas Sarwar Scotland not ready for a "brown, Muslim Paki"', *Daily Record*, 30 January 2018

Nick Cohen, 'The Left's Jewish Problem: Jeremy Corbyn, Israel and Anti-Semitism – Dave Rich's new history reveals the origins of Labour's recent antisemitic scandal in a wider leftwing revival of prejudice', *Guardian*, 13 September 2016

Norman Cohn, *Warrant for Genocide: The Myth of the Jewish World Conspiracy and the Protocols of the Elders of Zion* (London: Penguin, 1967)

Pippa Crerar and Heather Stewart, 'Labour acts against Margaret Hodge for calling Corbyn racist', *Guardian*, 18 July 2018

Lizzy Davies, 'France responsible for sending Jews to concentration camps, says court', *Guardian*, 17 February 2009

Alan Dershowitz, 'Do Jews Control the Media?', HuffPost, 6 October 2010

Wolfgang Dick, *'Antisemitismus spielt eine wesentliche Rolle bei der AfD: In Baden-Württemberg hat der Streit über antisemitisch eingestellte Mitglieder die AfD-Fraktion gepalten. Sozialwissenschaftler Jan Riebe wirft der AfD vor, sich zu wenig von antisemitischen Strömungen zu distanzieren'*, DW.com, 7 July 2016

Benjamin Disraeli, 'The Jewish Question is the Oriental Quest' (1877)

Benjamin Disraeli, N. H. Frankel & Theodor Herzl Gaster, *Unknown Documents on the Jewish Question: Disraeli's plan for a Jewish State* (1877) (Baltimore, MD and Tel-Aviv: Schlesinger Pub. Co., 1947)

Benjamin Disraeli Letters: 1852–1856, vol. VI, edited by Ann P. Robson, Mary S. Millar and M. G. Wiebe (Toronto: University of Toronto Press, 1997)

Uri Dromi, 'A Lib Dem and a blood libel', *Guardian*, 12 February 2010

Marcus Dysch, 'Baroness Royall report reveals Oxford Labour students engaged in antisemitism', *Jewish Chronicle*, 3 August 2016

George Eaton, 'Corbyn's "Zionist" remarks were "most offensive" since Enoch Powell, says ex-chief rabbi', *New Statesman*, 28 August 2018

A. Roy Eckardt, *Elder and Younger Brothers* (New York: Scribner, 1967)

___, *Your People, My People* (Chicago and New York: Quadrangle Books, 1974)

Charlotte Edwardes, 'Ruth Smeeth: "I've never seen anti-Semitism in Labour like this, it's normal now"', *Evening Standard*, 20 September 2016

John M. Efron, *Defenders of the Race: Jewish Doctors and Race Science in Fin-de-Siècle Europe* (London and New Haven: Yale University Press, 1994)

Akiva Eldar, 'U.S. State Department: Israel is not a tolerant society', *Ha'aretz*, 6 November 2009

Jessica Elgot, 'Labour accused of brushing aside alleged bias against Muslim women', *Guardian*, 6 February 2016

___, 'Chakrabarti: Ken Livingstone should no longer be in Labour party – Shadow attorney general says there are no circumstances under which disciplinary panel could not expel ex-mayor of London', *Guardian*, 13 May 2018

Amos Elon, *The Pity of It All: A History of the Jews in Germany, 1743–1933* (New York: Metropolitan Books, 2002), p. 108

Richard J. Evans, Expert Witness Report in Irving vs. (1) Lipstadt and (2) Penguin Books, 2000 https://phdn.org/negation/irving/EvansReport.pdf

___, *In Hitler's Shadow: West German Historians and the Attempt to Escape from the Nazi Past* (London: I. B. Tauris, 1989)

Emir Feisal, letter to Felix Frankfurter, amislam.com

Orlando Figes, *The Whisperers: Private Life in Stalin's Russia* (London: Allen Lane, 2007)

Daniel Finkelstein, 'Twitter's Holocaust denial', *Jewish Chronicle*, 7 April 2016

___, 'Anti-Semitism hasn't been an issue for me. Now it is', *The Times*, 21 August 2015

Josef Fraenkel, 'Louis D. Brandeis 1856–1941, Patriot, Judge, and Zionist', in The Rev. Dr Isaac Levy (ed.), *Makers of Modern Jewish History* (London: Education Committee of the Hillel Foundation, 17 March 2004)

Hadley Freeman, 'It's Jewish New Year, a time to eat and talk – and there'll only be one topic at the table', *Guardian*, 8 September 2018

Fundamental Rights Agency of the EU, 'Survey on discrimination and hate crime against Jews in EU', 2012, published 2013

___, 'Experiences and perceptions of antisemitism – Second survey on discrimination and hate crime against Jews in the EU', 2018

Martin Gilbert, *Kristallnacht: Prelude to Destruction* (London: HarperCollins, 2006)

Andrew Gilligan, 'Labour suspends official who blamed "all wars in the world" on Jewish people', *Sunday Times*, 16 December 2018

Ellen Goldberg, 'The New Israel Fund Says It's Time to Nail the Lies', open letter, 7 August 2009

Leo Goldberger, *The Rescue of the Danish Jews: Moral Courage Under Stress* (New York: NYU Press, 1988)

Lev Golinkin, 'America – and Judaism – at Its Best: The man accused of the synagogue massacre in Pittsburgh seemed fixated on HIAS, the refugee organization that helped save my family', *New York Times* opinion, 28 October 2018

Bruno Gollnisch, '*Négationnisme: Lyon III demande la suspension de Bruno Gollnisch*', *Le Nouvel Observateur*, 13 October 2004

Chris Green, 'Lord Sacks: Jewish people are thinking of leaving the UK in case Jeremy Corbyn becomes PM', *the i*, 2 September 2018, inews.co.uk/news/politics/lord-sacks-jewish

Peter Grose, 'Louis Brandeis, Arthur Balfour and a declaration that made history', *Moment Magazine* vol. 8, November 1983 , No. 10

Vasily Grossman, *Life and Fate* (London: Vintage Classic Russians Series, 2006)

Lee Harpin and Michael Daventry, 'Blair warns of Jew hate taking root in society', *Jewish Chronicle*, 11 May 2018

___, 'Board President Marie van der Zyl says rising antisemitism is "warning sign of genocide"', *Jewish Chronicle*, 5 November 2018

___, 'Huge crowds join Jewish community protest against antisemitism, in Westminster', *Jewish Chronicle*, 26 March 2018

Mehdi Hassan, 'The sorry truth is that the virus of anti-Semitism has infected the British Muslim community', *New Statesman*, 21 March 2013

Chris Hastings, 'Left-wing cyber trolls demand actress Maureen

Lipman is removed from *Coronation Street* after she called Jeremy Corbyn an "anti-Semite"', *Mail on Sunday*, 23 September 2018

Max Hastings, *Winston's War: Churchill, 1940–1945*, (London: Random House, 2011)

___, *The Secret War: Spies, Codes and Guerrillas 1939–1945* (London: William Collins, 2015)

Malcolm Hay, *Thy Brother's Blood: the Roots of Christian Anti-Semitism* (Oxford: Hart Publishing, 1975)

Jon Henley, 'Antisemitism on rise across Europe "in worst times since the Nazis" – Experts say attacks go beyond Israel-Palestinian conflict as hate crimes strike fear into Jewish communities', *Guardian*, 7 August 2014

___, 'Antisemitism rising sharply across Europe, latest figures show', *Guardian*, 15 February 2019

Theodor Herzl, *Der Judenstaat* (Leipzig and Vienna: Verlags-Buchhandlung, 1896)

___, *Altneuland* (Leipzig: Seemann Nachf, 1902)

Moses Hess, *Rome and Jerusalem* (New York: Bloch Publishing Company, 1918)

Christopher Hitchens, *Love, Poverty and War: Journeys and Essays* (New York: Nation Books, 2004)

___, *Hitch-22: A Memoir* (London: Atlantic Books, 2010)

Andrew Hussey, *The French Intifada* (London: Granta, 2014)

Paul Iganski and Barry Kosmin (eds.), *A New Antisemitism? Debating Judeophobia in 21st Century Britain* (London: Profile Books, 2003)

ITV Report, 'Margaret Hodge faces online backlash over Corbyn clash comparison', 17 August 2018, https://www.itv.com/news/2018-08-17/margaret-hodge-faces-online-backlash-over-corbyn-clash-comparison/

Steven L. Jacobs and Mark Weitzmann, *Dismantling the Big Lie: The Protocols of the Elders of Zion* (New York: KTAV Publishing House, 2003)

Jewish Telegraphic Agency, 'Jewish nurse said he showed empathy and compassion while caring for synagogue shooter', 4 November 2018

Charles C. Johnson, 'Thatcher and the Jews', *Tablet*, 28 December 2011

Lindsey Johnstone and AP, '"Yellow vests": Macron slams abuse of French philosopher Alain Finkielkraut at protests', *Euronews*, 17 February 2019

Mark Juergensmeyer, Margo Kitts and Michael Jerryson, *The Oxford Handbook of Religion and Violence* (Oxford: Oxford University Press, 2013)

Dominic Kennedy, 'Labour rising star Mohammed Pappu shared antisemitic posts on Facebook', *The Times*, 11 October 2018

Benjamin Kentish, 'Labour MPs condemn party leaders after admission that just 12 members have been expelled over antisemitism', *Independent*, 11 February 2019

Tom Kershaw, 'The International Paralympic Committee (IPC) has stripped Malaysia of its right to host the 2019 World Para Swimming Championships after the country upheld its ban on Israeli athletes participating', *Independent*, 28 January 2019

Benjamin Kerstein, 'Yes, all criticism of Israel is anti-Semitic', *Jerusalem Post*, 12 May 2012

Brian Klug, 'The left and the Jews: Labour's summer of discontent', *Jewish Quarterly*, 242 (Autumn 2018)

Walter Laqueur, *A History of Zionism: From the French Revolution to the Establishment of the State of Israel* (London: Penguin Random House, 2003)

———, *The Changing Face of Anti-Semitism: From Ancient Times to the Present Day* (New York: Oxford University Press, 2006)

Antony Lerman, 'Using Nazi analogies to criticise Israel or Zionism may be offensive, but should it be against the law?', *Guardian*, 24 July 2009

Bernard Lewis, 'The New Anti-Semitism', *The American Scholar*, Vol. 75, No. 1 (Winter 2006)

———, *The Jews of Islam* (Princeton: Princeton University Press, 1984)

———, *Semites and Anti-Semites: An Inquiry into Conflict and Prejudice* (New York: W. W. Norton & Co., 1999)

Deborah Lipstadt, *Antisemitism Here and Now* (London: Scribe, 2019)

Martin Luther, *On The Jews and Their Lies* (1543), transl. Martin H. Bertram, *Luther's Works*, Vol. 4 (Philadelphia: Fortress Press, 1971)

Jonathan Lynn letter, *The Times*, 25 August 2018

Sir William Macpherson, the Stephen Lawrence Inquiry Report, 1999

Kenneth Marcus, *The Definition of Anti-Semitism* (New York: Oxford University Press, 2016)

Rowena Mason and agency, 'Police arrest three in Labour anti-semitism case – Two men and a woman interviewed over antisemitic social media messages', *Guardian*, 28 March 2019

Caroline Moorehead, *Village of Secrets: Defying the Nazis in Vichy France* (London: Chatto and Windus, 2014)

Caroline Mortimer, 'Ken Livingstone fired from LBC show after Hitler comments trigger antisemitism row – The former Mayor of London is currently suspended from the Labour party for saying Hitler supported sending Jewish people to Israel', *Independent*, 28 May 2016

MSNBC, '50 Palestinians evicted from Jerusalem homes – Israeli police then allowed Jewish settlers to move into the houses', MSNBC, 2 August 2009

William Nicholls, *Christian Antisemitism: A History of Hate* (New York: Jason Aronson, 1993)

Barry Edward O'Meara, *Napoleon in Exile, or A Voice From St. Helena* (London: Simpkin and Marshall, 1822)

Susan Paley and Adrian Gibbons Koesters (compilers, eds.), A Viewer's Guide to Contemporary Passion Plays, prepared under the auspices of the Anti-Defamation League's Plains States Office, Creighton University (Omaha: University of Nebraska and Jewish Federation of Omaha, 2004)

James Parkes, *The Conflict of the Church and the Synagogue* (London: Soncino Press, 1934)

Stewart Paterson, 'One third of British Jews have considered quitting the UK because of anti-Semitic hate crimes reveals shock new survey', *Mailonline*, 20 August 2017

Daniella Peled, 'The Jewish Labour Gurus Striving to Turn Jeremy Corbyn's Reputation Around', *Ha'aretz*, 20 September 2016

The Pew Forum, 'Rising Tide of Restrictions on Religion', 20 September 2012, http://www.pewforum.org/2012/09/20/rising-tide-of-restrictions-on-religion-findings/

Barbara Pezzini, '"Rootless Cosmopolitans"? *Visual Resources*, an International Journal in Nationalist Times', 6 September 2017

Anshel Pfeffer, 'UK anti-Semitism Report Highlights Disturbing Trend Among British Jews: That over half of respondents compare the situation in Britain today with that of the 1930s shows a disconnect bordering on hysteria', *Ha'aretz*, 14 January 2015

Ariel Picard, 'Israel's Nationality Law will humiliate the Jews of the Diaspora', *JTA*, 18 July 2018

Leon Pinsker, *Autoemancipation!* (1882)

Leon Poliakov, *The History of Antisemitism* (4 vols) (New York: University of Pennsylvania Press, 1955–1984)

Stephen Pollard, 'There is only one word for Jeremy Corbyn – Mr Corbyn's explanation of his defence of an antisemitic mural is clearly untrue', *Jewish Chronicle*, 24 March 2018

Press TV, 'Belgian official: Israel steals organs of Palestinian kids', 21 October 2018

Peter Pulzer, *The Rise of Political Antisemitism* (London: Peter Halban Publishers Ltd, rev. edn 1988)

Barak Ravid, 'Merkel chides Netanyahu for failing to make "a single step to advance peace"', *Ha'aretz*, 25 February 2011

___, 'Veteran Israeli diplomat: Netanyahu and Lieberman harming Israel's stance in international community', *Ha'aretz*, 2 March 2011

Dave Rich, *The Left's Jewish Problem: Jeremy Corbyn, Israel and Anti-Semitism* (London: Biteback, 2016, rev. edn 2018)

Hugo Rifkind, 'Suddenly it feels uncomfortable to be a Jew', *The Times*, 12 August 2014

Rachel Riley, 'I thought the horror of the Shoah would mean no more antisemitism. I was wrong', *Jewish Chronicle*, 23 January 2019

Jeremy Rosen, 'Kaddish for Gaza', *Algemeiner Journal*, 22 June 2018

Yair Rosenberg, '"Jews will not replace us": Why white supremacists go after Jews', *Washington Post*, 14 August 2017

Kevin Sack, 'Transplant Brokers in Israel Lure Desperate Kidney Patients to Costa Rica', *New York Times*, 17 August 2014

Philippe Sands, *East West Street: On the Origins of Genocide and Crimes Against Humanity* (London: Weidenfeld & Nicolson, 2016)

Jean-Paul Sartre, *Anti-Semite and Jew: An Exploration of the Etiology of Hate* (London: Random House, 1995)

Simon Schama, Simon Sebag Montefiore and Howard Jacobson, letter to *The Times*, 6 November 2017

Charles A. Seldon, 'Prince of Hedjaz Welcomes Zionists', *New York Times*, 4 March 1919

Adam Sherwin, 'Danny Cohen: Jeremy Clarkson's nemesis', *Independent*, 27 March 2015

Harriet Sherwood, 'Rise in numbers of Jews leaving for Israel from some European countries – Institute of Jewish Policy Research says Jews are leaving some European countries in large numbers but says no parallels with 1930s can be drawn', *Guardian*, 12 January 2017

Harriet Sherwood, 'One in 20 Britons does not believe Holocaust took place, poll finds', *Observer*, 27 January 2019

Haroon Siddique, 'Ralph Miliband row: what the *Mail* said and how Ed Miliband responded', *Guardian*, 1 October 2013

Abe Silberstein, 'What the Nation-State Law Means, and What It Doesn't', Israel Policy Exchange, 24 July 2018

Brendan Simms and Charlie Laderman, 'The longest hatred: Anti-Semitism is resurgent in Europe. Can this ancient poison ever be eradicated?' *New Statesman*, 6–12 May, 2016

Sky News, 'Thousands join rival protests in Chemnitz, Germany, after man stabbed to death', 2 September 2018

Oli Smith, '"It is volatile" – German mayor issues "state of emergency" as Chemnitz violence escalates', *Express*, 3 September 2018

Marlon Solomon, 'Forget the Lizards: David Icke Is Dangerous and We Should Take Him Seriously', 4 January 2017 https://marlonsolomon.wordpress.com/2017/01/04/forget -the-lizards-david-icke-is-dangerous/

Jack Sommers, 'Theresa May's "Citizen of the World" View Blasted by *Financial Times* Reader – "I do understand very well what citizenship is, Mrs May"', HuffPost, 10 October 2016

Charles Spurgeon, *The restoration and conversion of the Jews*, no. 582, preached on Thursday evening, 16 June 1864, by the Rev. C. H. Spurgeon, at the Metropolitan Tabernacle, Newington, in aid of the Funds of the British Society for the Propagation of the Gospel among the Jews, *Metropolitan Tabernacle Pulpit* 1, Volume 10: 1

L. Daniel Staetsky, 'Antisemitism in contemporary Great Britain', Institute for Jewish Policy Research, London, 2017

___, 'Are Jews leaving Europe?' Institute for Jewish Policy Research report, London, 2017

Philip Stephens, 'Viktor Orbán's Hungary crosses to Europe's dark side – The campaign against George Soros digs up the demons of anti-Semitism', *Financial Times*, 13 July 2017

Danny Stone, 'Politicians Who Use Anti-Semitic Phrases Like "Cultural Marxism" Have A Duty To Explain Why', HuffPost, 29 March 2019

Daniel Sugarman, 'Conservative MEPs refuse to vote for EU action against "antisemitic" Hungarian government', *Jewish Chronicle*, 12 September 2018

James Tapsfield, Tim Sculthorpe and Matt Dathan, 'The extraordinary moment Labour MP John Mann branded Red Ken a "Nazi apologist" and "f****** disgrace" over claims Hitler backed moving the Jews to Israel "before he went mad and ended up killing six million Jews"', *Daily Mail*, 28 April 2016

Peter Walker, 'Labour investigates Liverpool members over "bullying" of Luciana Berger – Accusations of antisemitism follow no-confidence motion by Wavertree branch', *Observer*, 10 February 2019

Alison Weir, 'Israeli Organ Trafficking and Theft: From Moldova to Palestine', *Washington Report on Middle East Affairs*, November 2009

Ben Weich, 'Police Commissioner on Labour antisemitism dossier: "Small number" may be guilty of hate crime', *Jewish Chronicle*, 4 December 2018

___, 'Sebag Montefiore: "My duty is to speak out about antisemitism"', *Jewish Chronicle*, 12 October 2018

Arnold White, 'The Jewish Question: How to Solve It', *North American Review* 178 (566) (1904)

Sophie Wilkinson, 'How to beat hate', *Evening Standard*, 9 November 2018

Michael Wolffsohn, *Eternal Guilt? Forty Years of German-Jewish-Israeli Relations* (New York: Columbia University Press,1993)

Tomer Zarchin, 'Israeli Arabs More Likely to Be Convicted for Crimes than Their Jewish Counterparts, Study Shows', *Ha'aretz*, 2 August 2011

Alexander Zeldin, 'When Criticism of Israel Becomes Anti-Semitic', *Forward*, 11 December 2017

Émile Zola, *J'Accuse . . .!* (1898) (Paris: Mille et une nuits, 2003)

NOTES

Introduction

1 L Daniel Staetsky, 'Antisemitism in Contemporary Britain', Institute for Jewish Policy Research, London, 2017

Chapter One

1 Quoted in Malcolm Hay, *Thy Brother's Blood: the Roots of Christian Anti-Semitism* (Oxford: Hart Publishing, 1975)

2 Matthew: 27:25

3 Susan Paley and Adrian Gibbons Koesters (compilers, eds.), A Viewer's Guide to Contemporary Passion Plays, prepared under the auspices of the Anti-Defamation League's Plains States Office, Creighton University (Omaha: University of Nebraska and Jewish Federation of Omaha, 2004)

4 Michael Wolffsohn, *Eternal Guilt? Forty Years of German-Jewish-Israeli Relations* (New York: Columbia University Press, 1993), p. 194

5 Martin Luther, *On The Jews and Their Lies* (1543), transl. Martin H. Bertram, *Luther's Works*, Vol. 4 (Philadelphia: Fortress Press, 1971).

6 Amos Elon, *The Pity of It All: A History of the Jews in Germany, 1743–1933* (New York: Metropolitan Books, 2002), p. 108

7 Bernard Lewis, 'The New Anti-Semitism', *The American Scholar*, Vol. 75, No. 1 (Winter 2006), pp. 25–36; based on a lecture delivered at Brandeis University on 24 March 2004

8 Lee Harpin, 'Board President Marie van der Zyl says rising antisemitism is "warning sign of genocide"', *Jewish Chronicle*, 5 November 2018

9 Ibid.

10 Bernard Lewis, *The Jews of Islam* (Princeton: Princeton University Press, 1984), and Bernard Lewis, *Semites and Anti-Semites: An Inquiry into Conflict and Prejudice* (New York: W. W. Norton & Co., 1999)

11 Paragraph 16

12 4:157: 'they [Jews] killed him [Jesus] not'

13 2:61

14 5:69

15 Quoted in Laqueur, *The Changing Face of Antisemitism*, p. 192

16 Mark Juergensmeyer, Margo Kitts and Michael Jerryson, *The Oxford Handbook of Religion and Violence* (Oxford: Oxford University Press, 2013), p. 484

17 Norman Cohn, *Warrant for Genocide: The Myth of the Jewish World Conspiracy and the Protocols of the Elders of Zion* (London: Penguin, 1967)

18 Steven L. Jacobs and Mark Weitzman, *Dismantling the Big Lie: The Protocols of the Elders of Zion* (New York: KTAV Publishing House, 2003), p. xi

19 Despite arguments about the authenticity of him saying this, the speech is published on Hezbollah's website moqawama.org

20 Brendan Simms and Charlie Laderman, 'The longest hatred: Anti-Semitism is resurgent in Europe. Can this ancient poison ever be eradicated?' *New Statesman*, 6–12 May 2016

21 David Aaronovitch, 'The new anti-Semitism. A document once used by the Nazis to stir up hatred of Jews and long known to be a forgery is once again being circulated, this time by Muslim scholars', *Observer*, 22 June 2003

22 'Malaysian leader says anti-Semitism "invented to prevent criticism of Jews"', AP, *Times of Israel*, 16 August 2018

23 Tom Kershaw, 'The International Paralympic Committee (IPC) has stripped Malaysia of its right to host the 2019 World Para Swimming Championships after the country upheld its ban on Israeli athletes participating', *Independent*, 28 January 2019

24 Mehdi Hassan, 'The sorry truth is that the virus of anti-Semitism has infected the British Muslim community', *New Statesman*, 21 March 2013

25 John M. Efron, *Defenders of the Race: Jewish Doctors and Race Science in Fin-de-Siècle Europe* (London and New Haven: Yale University Press, 1994)

26 Recommendation 12 of the Stephen Lawrence Inquiry Report by Sir William Macpherson, 1999

27 *Daily Telegraph*, 12 November 1938. Cited in Martin Gilbert, *Kristallnacht: Prelude to Destruction* (London: HarperCollins, 2006), p. 142

28 See A. Roy Eckardt, *Elder and Younger Brothers* (New York: Scribner, 1967); A. Roy Eckardt, *Your People, My People* (Chicago and New York: Quadrangle Books), 1974

29 Yair Rosenberg, '"Jews will not replace us": Why white supremacists go after Jews', *Washington Post*, 14 August 2017

30 The declaration was the outcome of the International Forum convened in Stockholm from 27–29 January 2000 by former Swedish Prime Minister Göran Persson, and attended by the representatives of 46 governments

31 Kenneth Marcus, *The Definition of Anti-Semitism* (New York: Oxford University Press, 2016)

32 Walter Laqueur, *The Changing Face of Anti-Semitism: From Ancient Times to the Present Day* (New York: Oxford University Press, 2006)

Chapter Two

1 There are many histories of Zionism, among which Walter Laqueur's masterly *A History of Zionism: From the French Revolution to the Establishment of the State of Israel* (London: Penguin Random House, 2003) is probably the most thorough and useful

2 'History of the national question in Russia at Russian Committee in defense of the human rights' (in Russian), and in Levon Chorbajian and George Shirinian (eds.), *Studies in Comparative Genocide* (Basingstoke: Palgrave Macmillan, 1999)

3 Arnold White, 'The Jewish Question: How to Solve It', *North American Review* 178 (566) (1904), pp. 10–24

4 Moses Hess, *Rome and Jerusalem* (New York: Bloch Publishing Company, 1918) https://archive.org/details/romeandjerusale02waxmgoog/ also Wikisource: https://en.wikisource.org/wiki/Rome_and_Jerusalem

5 Leon Pinsker, *Autoemancipation!* (1882), www.thefullwiki.org/Auto-Emancipation http://www.geocities.com/Vienna/6640/zion/pinsker.html

6 Charles Spurgeon, *The restoration and conversion of the Jews*, no. 582, preached on Thursday evening, 16 June 1864, by the Rev. C. H. Spurgeon, at the Metropolitan Tabernacle, Newington, in aid of the Funds of the British Society for the Propagation of the Gospel among the Jews, *Metropolitan Tabernacle Pulpit* 1, Volume 10: 1

7 *Benjamin Disraeli Letters: 1852–1856*, vol. VI, edited by Ann P. Robson, Mary S. Millar and M. G. Wiebe (Toronto: University of Toronto Press, 1997)

8 Benjamin Disraeli, N. H. Frankel and Theodor Herzl Gaster, *Unknown Documents on the Jewish Question: Disraeli's plan for a Jewish State* (1877) (Baltimore, MD and Tel-Aviv: Schlesinger Pub. Co., 1947)

9 Émile Zola, *J'Accuse . . .!* (1898) (Paris: Mille et une nuits, 2003)

10 'Zionism-Israel Information Center Historical Source Documents – Edwin Montagu Memorandum on the Balfour Declaration as Antisemitism, August 1917 Judaism and Zionism'. www.zionism-israel.com

11 Josef Fraenkel, 'Louis D. Brandeis 1856–1941, Patriot, Judge, and Zionist', in The Rev. Dr Isaac Levy (ed.), *Makers of Modern Jewish History* (London: Education Committee of the Hillel Foundation, 17 March 2004)

12 Letter by Emir Feisal to Felix Frankfurter, published in full at amislam.com (collection of correspondence) and Charles A Seldon, 'Prince of Hedjaz Welcomes Zionists', *New York Times*, 4 March 1919, Paris

13 Benjamin Kerstein, 'Yes, all criticism of Israel is anti-Semitic', *Jerusalem Post*, 12 May 2012

14 Alexander Zeldin, 'When Criticism of Israel Becomes Anti-Semitic', *Forward*, 11 December 2017, https://forward.com/scribe/389823/when-criticism-of-israel-becomes-anti-semitic/

15 Ibid

16 Abe Silberstein, 'What the Nation-State Law Means, and What It Doesn't', Israel Policy Exchange, 24 July 2018

17 Ian Black, 'Doctor admits Israeli pathologists harvested organs without consent', *Guardian*, 21 December 2009

18 Donald Boström, '"Our sons are plundered of their organs" – Palestinians accuse the Israel Defense Forces of taking organs from their victims', *Aftonbladet*, 26 August 2009

19 Alison Weir, 'Israeli Organ Trafficking and Theft: From Moldova to Palestine', *Washington Report on Middle East Affairs*,

November 2009, pp. 15–17, https://ifamericaknew.org/cur_sit/aw-organs2.html

20 AlisonWeir.org – Journal – Israeli organ harvesting? alisonweir.org/journal/.../9/1/israeli-organ-harvesting.html

21 'Belgian official: Israel steals organs of Palestinian kids', 21 October 2018, https://www.presstv.com/detail/2018/10/21/577649/israel-organ-harvesting-belgian-official

22 Kevin Sack, 'Transplant Brokers in Israel Lure Desperate Kidney Patients to Costa Rica', *New York Times*, 17 August 2014

23 Uri Dromi, 'A Lib Dem and a blood libel', *Guardian*, 12 February 2010

24 Akiva Eldar, 'U.S. State Department: Israel is not a tolerant society', *Ha'aretz*, 6 November 2009

25 The Pew Forum, 'Rising Tide of Restrictions on Religion', 20 September 2012, http://www.pewforum.org/2012/09/20/rising-tide-of-restrictions-on-religion-findings/

26 Jonathan Adelman, 'The Christians of Israel: A Remarkable Group', HuffPost, 28 August 2015 (updated 28 August 2016)

27 See for example 'Palestinians evicted in Jerusalem', BBC News, 2 August 2009; '50 Palestinians evicted from Jerusalem homes – Israeli police then allowed Jewish settlers to move into the houses', MSNBC, 2 August 2009

28 The Or Commission, chaired by Theodore Or, an Israeli Supreme Court judge, was set up to investigate the events of October 2000, at the beginning of the second Intifada, when 12 Arab citizens of Israel and one Palestinian were killed by Israeli police at various demonstrations. The inquiry criticised the Israeli police for being unprepared for the riots and using excessive force to disperse protesting and rioting citizens. Eight policemen were reprimanded by the commission. But what was significant was that the Or Commission found that Arab citizens suffer discrimination in Israel and criticised the government for failing to give fair and equal attention to the needs of Arab citizens of Israel. The commission also found that frustration with discrimination led to the outpourings in riots in October 2000.

29 Tomer Zarchin, 'Israeli Arabs More Likely to Be Convicted for Crimes than Their Jewish Counterparts, Study Shows', *Ha'aretz*, 2 August 2011

30 Jon Henley, 'Antisemitism on rise across Europe "in worst times since the Nazis" – Experts say attacks go beyond

Israel-Palestinian conflict as hate crimes strike fear into Jewish communities', *Guardian*, 7 August 2014

31 Ofer Aderet, 'Anti-Semitism Growing Among Far Right and Muslim Migrants in Germany, State Premier Tells *Haaretz*', *Ha'aretz*, 3 September 2018

32 Jon Henley, 'Antisemitism rising sharply across Europe, latest figures show', *Guardian*, 15 February 2019

33 Sky News, 'Thousands join rival protests in Chemnitz, Germany, after man stabbed to death', 2 September 2018

34 Oli Smith, '"It is volatile" – German mayor issues "state of emergency" as Chemnitz violence escalates', *Express*, 3 September 2018; see also Henley, 'Antisemitism on rise across Europe "in worst times since the Nazis"', 7 August 2014: 'Germany's chancellor, Angela Merkel, has called recent incidents "an attack on freedom and tolerance and our democratic state"'

35 Wolfgang Dick, '*Antisemitismus spielt eine wesentliche Rolle bei der AfD: In Baden-Württemberg hat der Streit über antisemitisch eingestellte Mitglieder die AfD-Fraktion gepalten. Sozialwissenschaftler Jan Riebe wirft der AfD vor, sich zu wenig von antisemitischen Strömungen zu distanzieren*', DW.com, 7 July 2016

36 In defence of citizens of the world pic.twitter.com/YQQXP6gf05 — Henry Mance (@henrymance), 10 October 2016

37 Jack Sommers, 'Theresa May's "Citizen of the World" View Blasted by *Financial Times* Reader – "I do understand very well what citizenship is, Mrs May"', HuffPost, 10 October 2016

38 This is dealt with in detail in a variety of books, but spectacularly well in S. W. Baron, *A Social and Religious History of the Jews*, 18 vols. (New York: Columbia University Press, 1952–83)

39 Orlando Figes, *The Whisperers: Private Life in Stalin's Russia* (London: Allen Lane, 2007)

40 Barbara Pezzini, '"Rootless Cosmopolitans"? *Visual Resources*, an International Journal in Nationalist Times', 6 September 2017, https://doi.org/10.1080/01973762.2017.1358568

41 Nathanael Kapner, http://www.targetfreedomusa.com/timeline-and-history-of-jewish-domination/ or http://www.realjewnews.com/?p=140

42 https://cst.org.uk/news/blog/2018/12/20/eu-survey-what-do-british-jews-consider-to-be-antisemitic

43 Alan Dershowitz, 'Do Jews Control the Media?', HuffPost, 6 October 2010

44 James Carroll, 'One Cardinal's Old Impulse to Blame Jews', *Boston Globe*, 13 August 2003

45 Harriet Sherwood, 'One in 20 Britons does not believe Holocaust took place, poll finds', *Observer*, 27 January 2019

46 Daniel Finkelstein, 'Twitter's Holocaust denial', *Jewish Chronicle*, 7 April 2016

47 Twitter, Replying to @askhistorians7:25 PM 18 July 2018

48 Irving vs. (1) Lipstadt and (2) Penguin Books, Expert Witness Report by Richard J. Evans FBA, Professor of Modern History, University of Cambridge, 2000, Chapter 6: Conclusion, starting p. 726, in: Irving vs. (1) Lipstadt and (2) Penguin Books pdf p. 377, https://phdn.org/negation/irving/EvansReport.pdf

49 Christopher Hitchens, 'The Strange Case of David Irving', *Los Angeles Times*, 20 May 2001. Reprinted in Christopher Hitchens, *Love, Poverty and War: Journeys and Essays* (New York: Nation Books, 2004), p. 261

50 Marlon Solomon blog, 'Forget the Lizards: David Icke Is Dangerous and We Should Take Him Seriously', 4 January 2017, https://marlonsolomon.wordpress.com/2017/01/04/forget-the-lizards-david-icke-is-dangerous/

51 David Icke (Critical Thinking), 'From BBC to PCT', © 2004, http://www.critical-thinking.org.uk/conspiracy-theories/david-icke.php

52 Richard J. Evans, *In Hitler's Shadow: West German Historians and the Attempt to Escape from the Nazi Past* (London: I. B. Tauris, 1989)

53 Bruno Gollnisch, '*Négationnisme: Lyon III demande la suspension de Bruno Gollnisch*', *Le Nouvel Observateur*, 13 October 2004

54 *Je l'avais connu et que c'était un homme bien*' – 'I knew him and he was a good man', '*L'antisémitisme ordinaire ou les dérapages de Raymond Barre*', Zapping radio, 13 March 2007

55 BBC News, 'Nazi stag-do Tory MP Aidan Burley to step down', 5 February 2014

56 Margaret Thatcher, quoted in Charles C. Johnson, 'Thatcher and the Jews', *Tablet*, 28 December 2011, Tabletmag.com https://www.tabletmag.com/jewish-news-and-politics/87027/thatcher-and-the-jews

57 Ibid

58 Alan Connor, 'Top of the class', BBC News, 17 October 2005, http://news.bbc.co.uk/1/hi/magazine/4349324.stm

59 Philip Stephens, 'Viktor Orbán's Hungary crosses to Europe's dark side – The campaign against George Soros digs up the demons of anti-Semitism', *Financial Times*, 13 July 2017

60 Daniel Sugarman, 'Conservative MEPs refuse to vote for EU action against "antisemitic" Hungarian government', *Jewish Chronicle*, 12 September 2018

61 Quoted in Lizzy Buchan, 'Tory MEPs ordered to distance themselves from Hungary's far-right Viktor Orbán after vote controversy', *Independent*, 13 September 2018

62 'Islamophobia claims in Conservative party: Warsi on May', BBC News, 5 March 2019, https://www.bbc.co.uk/news/av/uk-politics-47460240/islamophobia-claims-in-conservative-party-warsi-on-may

63 RT.com, 'UK Islamophobic incidents soar 600% in week after Christchurch terrorist attacks', 25 March 2019, https://www.rt.com/uk/454681-muslim-hate-increase-christchurch/

64 Caroline Mortimer, 'Ken Livingstone fired from LBC show after Hitler comments trigger antisemitism row – The former Mayor of London is currently suspended from the Labour party for saying Hitler supported sending Jewish people to Israel', *Independent*, 28 May 2016

65 Jessica Elgot, 'Chakrabarti: Ken Livingstone should no longer be in Labour party – Shadow attorney general says there are no circumstances under which disciplinary panel could not expel ex-mayor of London', *Guardian*, 13 May 2018

66 James Tapsfield, Tim Sculthorpe and Matt Dathan, 'The extraordinary moment Labour MP John Mann branded Red Ken a "Nazi apologist" and "f****** disgrace" over claims Hitler backed moving the Jews to Israel "before he went mad and ended up killing six million Jews"', *Daily Mail*, 28 April 2016

67 This emerged in a conversation between the author and Mark Gardner, deputy CEO and director of communications at the Community Security Trust (CST), 4 February 2019

68 Jonathan Freedland, 'My plea to the left: treat Jews the same way you'd treat any other minority', *Guardian*, 29 April 2016

69 Camilla Turner, 'Oxford University's Labour Club embroiled in anti-Semitism row', *Telegraph*, 16 February 2016

70 Aftab Ali, 'Oxford University Labour Club students did engage in anti-Semitic behaviour, report finds', *Independent*, 3 August 2016; Marcus Dysch, 'Baroness Royall report reveals Oxford

Labour students engaged in antisemitism', *Jewish Chronicle*, 3 August 2016

71 Liz Bates and Kevin Schofield, 'Labour councillor suspended over "Jews drink blood and rape children" social media post', *PoliticsHome*, 27 July 2018

72 Andrew Gilligan, 'Labour suspends official who blamed "all wars in the world" on Jewish people', *Sunday Times*, 16 December 2018

73 Quoted in Daniella Peled, 'The Jewish Labour Gurus Striving to Turn Jeremy Corbyn's Reputation Around', *Ha'aretz*, 20 September 2016

74 Charlotte Edwardes, 'Ruth Smeeth: "I've never seen anti-Semitism in Labour like this, it's normal now"', *Evening Standard*, 20 September 2016

75 Brian Klug, 'The left and the Jews: Labour's summer of discontent', *Jewish Quarterly*, 242 (Autumn 2018)

76 Chris Hastings, 'Left-wing cyber trolls demand actress Maureen Lipman is removed from *Coronation Street* after she called Jeremy Corbyn an "anti-Semite"', *Mail on Sunday*, 23 September 2018

77 Pippa Crerar and Heather Stewart, 'Labour acts against Margaret Hodge for calling Corbyn racist', *Guardian*, 18 July 2018

78 ITV Report, 'Margaret Hodge faces online backlash over Corbyn clash comparison', 17 August 2018, https://www.itv.com/news/2018-08-17/margaret-hodge-faces-online-backlash-over-corbyn-clash-comparison/

79 Ben Weich, 'Police Commissioner on Labour antisemitism dossier: "Small number" may be guilty of hate crime', *Jewish Chronicle*, 4 December 2018

80 Rowena Mason and agency, 'Police arrest three in Labour antisemitism case – Two men and a woman interviewed over antisemitic social media messages', *Guardian*, 28 March 2019

81 Dominic Kennedy, 'Labour rising star Mohammed Pappu shared antisemitic posts on Facebook', *The Times*, 11 October 2018

82 Daniel Martin, 'Labour fury as it emerges Jeremy Corbyn once defended "anti-Semitic" public mural showing a group of "hook-nosed" men around a Monopoly board', Mailonline, 24 March 2018

83 See http://labourbriefing.squarespace.com/home/2018/8/29/full-texxt-of-that-speech-by-jeremy-on-zionists-and-a-sense-of-irony

84 George Eaton, 'Corbyn's "Zionist" remarks were "most offensive" since Enoch Powell, says ex-chief rabbi', *New Statesman*, 28 August 2018

85 Chris Green, 'Lord Sacks: Jewish people are thinking of leaving the UK in case Jeremy Corbyn becomes PM', *the i*, 2 September 2018, inews.co.uk/news/politics/lord-sacks-jewish

86 Jonathan Lynn letter, *The Times*, 25 August 2018

87 Peter Walker, 'Labour investigates Liverpool members over "bullying" of Luciana Berger – Accusations of antisemitism follow no-confidence motion by Wavertree branch', *Observer*, 10 February 2019

88 Benjamin Kentish, 'Labour MPs condemn party leaders after admission that just 12 members have been expelled over antisemitism', *Independent*, 11 February 2019

89 Richard Kerbaj, Gabriel Pogrund, Tom Calver, 'Vile anti-Semitism met with "a slap on the wrist at most"', The Labour Files, *Sunday Times*, 7 April 2019

90 Leader: *Sunday Times*, 7 April 2019

91 AFP news.france@thelocal.com, 'Why 5000 Jews emigrated from France to Israel last year', AFP, 9 January 2017, https://www.thelocal.fr/20170109/5000-more-jews-leave-france-for-israel

92 Andrew Hussey, *The French Intifada* (London: Granta, 2014), p. 27

93 *Algemeiner* staff, 'Jewish Owned Stores Burned to the Ground, Synagogue Firebombed in "Paris Intifada"', *Algemeiner*, 21 July 2014

94 Lindsey Johnstone and AP, '"Yellow vests": Macron slams abuse of French philosopher Alain Finkielkraut at protests', *Euronews*, 17 February 2019

95 L. Daniel Staetsky, 'Are Jews leaving Europe?' Institute for Jewish Policy Research report (London, 2017)

96 Harriet Sherwood, 'Rise in numbers of Jews leaving for Israel from some European countries – Institute of Jewish Policy Research says Jews are leaving some European countries in large numbers but says no parallels with 1930s can be drawn', *Guardian*, 12 January 2017

97 Gab says it has 'zero tolerance' for terrorism and violence, but alt-right and Holocaust deniers and racists meet on its site

98 Lev Golinkin, 'America – and Judaism – at Its Best: The man accused of the synagogue massacre in Pittsburgh seemed fixated on HIAS, the refugee organization that helped save my family', *New York Times* opinion, 28 October 2018

99 Ibid

100 Jacob Sugarman, 'Has Donald Trump Made the World Less

Safe for Jews?' AlterNet, 19 April 2018, https://www.alternet.
org/2018/04/has-donald-trump-made-world-less-safe-jews/
101 Jewish Telegraphic Agency, 'Jewish nurse said he showed
empathy and compassion while caring for synagogue shooter', 4
November 2018

Chapter Three

1 Lee Harpin, 'Huge crowds join Jewish community protest
against antisemitism, in Westminster', *Jewish Chronicle*, 26 March
2018
2 Danny Stone, 'Politicians Who Use Anti-Semitic Phrases Like
"Cultural Marxism" Have A Duty To Explain Why', HuffPost,
29 March 2019
3 Rachel Riley, 'I thought the horror of the Shoah would mean
no more antisemitism. I was wrong', *Jewish Chronicle*, 23 January
2019, https://www.thejc.com/news/uk-news/rachel-riley-speech-
holocaust-educational-trust-1.479017; Twitter, https://twitter.
com/rachelrileyrr/status/1087823875713445896?s=21
4 Rod Ardehali, '"I can't thank people enough for seeing through
the lies": *Countdown*'s Rachel Riley praises fans for their support
after slamming Corbyn and telling George Galloway to f*** off
in anti-Semitism row', Mailonline, 10 January 2019
5 'Was Roald Dahl antisemitic?' *The Week*, UK, 7 November 2018
6 Deborah Lipstadt, *Antisemitism Here and Now* (London: Scribe,
2019)
7 Hugo Rifkind, 'Suddenly it feels uncomfortable to be a Jew', *The
Times*, 12 August 2014
8 Daniel Finkelstein, 'Anti-Semitism hasn't been an issue for me.
Now it is', *The Times*, 21 August 2015
9 Ben Weich, 'Sebag Montefiore: "My duty is to speak out about
antisemitism"', *Jewish Chronicle*, 12 October 2018
10 *Telegraph* Sport: '"Yid" chanting by Tottenham Hotspur fans no
longer an arrestable offence at White Hart Lane says Met Police',
Daily Telegraph, 18 June 2014
11 Anshel Pfeffer, *Ha'aretz*, 14 January 2015
12 L. Daniel Staetsky, 'Antisemitism in contemporary Great Britain',
Institute for Jewish Policy Research, London 2017
13 This 'elastic view' is supported by Deborah Lipstadt in her
excellent book *Antisemitism Here and Now*

14 Dave Rich, *The Left's Jewish Problem: Jeremy Corbyn, Israel and Anti-Semitism* (London: Biteback, 2016, rev. edn 2018)

15 Nick Cohen, 'The Left's Jewish Problem: Jeremy Corbyn, Israel and Anti-Semitism – Dave Rich's new history reveals the origins of Labour's recent antisemitic scandal in a wider leftwing revival of prejudice', *Guardian*, 13 September 2016

16 FRA (Fundamental Rights Agency of the EU), 'Survey on discrimination and hate crime against Jews in EU', 2012, published 2013; FRA, 'Experiences and perceptions of antisemitism – Second survey on discrimination and hate crime against Jews in the EU', 2018

17 Hadley Freeman, 'It's Jewish New Year, a time to eat and talk – and there'll only be one topic at the table', *Guardian*, 8 September 2018

18 Quoted in Sophie Wilkinson, 'How to beat hate', *Evening Standard*, 9 November 2018

19 Lee Harpin and Michael Daventry, 'Blair warns of Jew hate taking root in society', *Jewish Chronicle*, 11 May 2018

20 David Clegg, 'Labour suspend councillor over claims he told Anas Sarwar Scotland not ready for a "brown, Muslim Paki"', *Daily Record*, 30 January 2018; Jessica Elgot, 'Labour accused of brushing aside alleged bias against Muslim women', *Guardian*, 6 February 2016

21 Adam Sherwin, 'Danny Cohen: Jeremy Clarkson's nemesis', *Independent*, 27 March 2015

22 Haroon Siddique, 'Ralph Miliband row: what the *Mail* said and how Ed Miliband responded', *Guardian*, 1 October 2013

23 Christopher Hitchens, *Hitch-22: A Memoir* (London: Atlantic Books, 2010)

24 Christopher Hitchens and Martin Amis in conversation, Jewish Book Week 2007, www.youtube.com/watch?v=0KxEFqs9yRg

25 Vasily Grossman, *Life and Fate* (London: Vintage Classic Russians Series, 2006)

26 There are several versions. See https://en.wikipedia.org/wiki/First_they_came_...